MAKE YOUR MARRIAGE WORK:
LOVING WITH PURPOSE

MAKE YOUR MARRIAGE WORK: LOVING WITH PURPOSE

Matt Alley

For more information about our products or services, please visit MattAlleyMinistries.com or contact the author via email at matt@mattalleyministries.com

Publishers Cataloging-in-Publication Data

Make Your Marriage Work: Loving with Purpose

pages 118 cm.

ISBN: 978-1-7345297-0-8 paperback
    978-1-7345297-1-5 ePUB
    978-1-7345297-2-2 MOBI

Printed in the United States of America

Dedication

I would like to dedicate this book to my wonderful wife, Erin, and my two incredible kids, Mattie and Jase.

Table of Contents

Foreword

There are two things in life that I really hate (and yes I know 'hate' is a strong word). The short list consists of cilantro and spiders. They make me sick and terrified, respectively.

There are also two things in life I love (to be fair, there are more than two, but these two come to mind). I love books. And I love marriage.

I love reading books and I love writing books. I love my marriage. I love teaching about marriage and writing about marriage and learning about marriage. So when my dear friend and brother, Matt Alley, asked me to read his new book on marriage, just imagine my anticipation! I love books and I love marriage, so this was a double-win for me. If I'm being honest, however, I was taken off-guard by just how good this book is.

I've read many books on marriage. I've even written a few. But this one is different. It's special. I know Matt and his wife, and I know their story of redemption, forgiveness, and restoration. But there is something about reading it on a page that hits a deep place in my soul. Matt writes with great clarity, but also with tremendous vulnerability. He tells his true story, the good and the bad, but refuses to wallow in the mistakes that were made.

Instead, he paints a beautiful picture of what God can do when a husband and wife come to the end of themselves and totally surrender to Jesus.

One thing I love about this book is the realistic way in which Matt shows us how easy it is to get sidetracked, but also how faithful God is to restore and redeem. Matt is a pastor, but even pastors are vulnerable to the pitfalls that shipwreck so many marriages. The end result for the Alleys is now a stronger marriage, a deeper love for each other and Jesus, and a powerful testimony that is helping others find hope in seemingly hopeless marriages.

The book also tackles big relationship issues with simple, practical truth. It answers questions like why marriage matters, where marriage comes from, and the ultimate reason behind God's creation of the marriage relationship in the first place. According to Matt, marriage exists for intimacy, children, companionship, and God's glory. When we rightly prioritize our relationships with Christ at the center, we will have the Spirit-enabled endurance that we need to make it to the finish line, hand-in-hand with our mate.

The book makes the case, clearly and biblically, that the secret to contentment is not a marriage relationship, but a relationship with Jesus Christ. So if I were you, I would dive into this book right now. Clear a few hours on your calendar, get a cup of coffee (or tea, if that's more your speed), and get ready to be challenged, encouraged, and equipped to have the best marriage you could possibly experience. Isn't that what a good Heavenly Father would want for His children that He dearly loves?

I'm so thankful for this book, and I know you will be as well.

–Clayton King

Acknowledgements

I want to thank the following people for helping me accomplish a dream of mine, that I hope will help thousands of people and marriages: Erin Alley, Jordan and Amanda Green, Sam and Sara Alley, Keith and Donna Sheppard, Samantha and Jordan Evans, Tony and Janet Tench, my Friday morning men's group, and the wonderful Greenwood Campus of NewSpring Church and our staff: Tyler Smith, Holly Cox, Shannon Mountz, Donna Gilmer, Nate Liverman, Tommy and Haley Lasley, and Matt Buckland.

Chapter 1

My Story

I had a pretty typical upbringing for the south. I was born in Albemarle, NC, and then my family moved to Roxboro, NC, before finally settling in Anderson, SC. We moved because of my dad taking jobs that would pay more money, or so I thought. We were a family who prioritized church, but not so much individual relationships with Jesus. My dad was always a deacon, chairman of some committee or another, and my mom was always in the choir or on the praise team. We were at church every Sunday, every Wednesday, and sometimes on days in between. However, I never remember seeing either of my parents open their Bibles for the purpose of growing a personal relationship with Jesus Christ.

We were also a family who prioritized sports over anything else, including time together. I don't remember us sitting down for many meals together at home (it didn't help that my mom couldn't cook), or just sitting in the living room enjoying each other's company, playing games, or anything of the sort. We were always at a baseball or softball field or a basketball court. We spent a lot of time traveling with the different teams that my sister and I were on. We were a typical, southern family that prioritized church and sports, but left Jesus out of the equation most of the time.

I gave my life to Jesus at Lamberth Memorial Baptist Church in Roxboro, NC when I was 9 years old. I had been asking a lot of questions about putting my faith in Jesus, so my parents talked to our pastor, Dr. Jim McCoy, and he agreed to spend some time with me. After spending time together talking, Dr. McCoy answering my questions, and going through a workbook with him, I gave my life to Jesus on the steps of that church. I was baptized the week after, and that was when everything changed for me. I took my relationship with Jesus very seriously, from reading the Bible to going to church. I felt like God had something in store for my life that would involve Him and His Church.

We moved to Anderson, SC not too long after that. After settling down at First Baptist Church of Anderson, I began to get deeply involved in everything church and Jesus related. I bought all the shirts that were knock-off designs of major brands but had some kind of corny Jesus-saying on them, and I was "all in." The only thing I was focused on for the rest of middle and high school was Jesus, school, and sports. I was "Mr. Youth Choir" in middle school, and through high school climbed the ranks of the youth group offices (or the youth group popularity contest), from secretary to vice-president to president. When not at church, I was usually on the basketball court. I was also focused on making good grades, although in high school I didn't have to put in very much effort for that to happen.

It was during these high school years that God made it clear to me that I was supposed to go into ministry full-time. I was on a trip with my youth group during New Year's Eve and New Year's Day of 1999/2000. On New Year's Eve during a time of worship and preaching, I felt God speak to my heart. I'd always had a gift and passion for teaching and speaking in public, and I had been told that I was a very compassionate and sympathetic person. Now, it seemed that God wanted to use those things for His glory, my joy, and the good of others.

I came back from that trip full of excitement, enthusiasm, and zeal for God, for His Church, and for what He wanted to do in and through me. I shared the news about what had happened to me on that trip with my family, friends, and anyone who seemed at all interested. Unfortunately, my enthusiasm and excitement weren't met with the same reaction from others around me.

I was told that I was too intelligent for vocational ministry, that my talents for math and science would be wasted and unused by going into vocational ministry, and therefore I was doing God, my family, and others a disservice by not using those things. I was told that I would never make enough money in vocational ministry to support a family and provide for my future spouse and kids like I had the potential of doing if I did something else.

It was then that I caved into peer pressure from others and went a different direction than what God had called me to. I decided to go to Clemson University and major in engineering. I went through my first semester and decided that I wasn't interested in any of the disciplines of engineering, and that lack of interest combined with the bad decisions I made from joining a fraternity led to a very academically-unsuccessful first semester.

I switched to being a math major (to bring my GPA up), and then eventually became a Secondary Education Math major and a manager for Clemson's basketball team under Oliver Purnell. My plans then were to teach high school math and be a high school basketball coach, and maybe eventually work my way up to being a college basketball coach. Then the summer of 2005 happened, and everything changed...

It was a Saturday morning. I had just come home from Clemson for the summer, and my sister graduated high school the night before. I woke up to the smell of cinnamon rolls as I normally did on Saturday mornings at our house. I walked into the living room and noticed that both of my parents were sitting on the couch, mom had been crying and dad looked frustrated and hurt. They asked me to go get my sister out of bed and bring her into the living room. I went and woke her from her hangover-induced sleep and we went into the living room together.

My parents then told us something that completely blindsided me: they were getting separated. Mom was moving out, after a year they would be officially divorced, and that it was unmendable. They had committed to waiting until my sister and I were both done with high school, and I guess they were so ready they decided to wait only 12 hours after Samantha's graduation. This news completely took me by surprise, and I can't explain how angry I was. I hit a couple of walls, slammed the door, and drove around for what seemed like days!

My parents said they had "irreconcilable differences," that they had nothing in common, and for those reasons they weren't going to spend the rest of their lives being miserable. Years later I found out it was actually because my mom had made a lot of bad decisions, which was why we moved to three different cities, and ultimately why my parents divorced. The woman I trusted more than anyone had let my dad down, had let me down, and had let my family down. A marriage I thought was thriving wasn't even surviving, and that's when I vowed that a failed marriage would never happen to me. The Bible tells us:

> *We know that all things work together for the good of those who love God, who are called according to His purpose.*
> –Romans 8:28 (CSB)

While I had no clue why this was happening to my family, I had to lean into the promises of God that I knew were true, including this one. That summer, I leaned into this promise and began soul-searching. I dug into Scripture and my relationship with God like never before, because I knew that He was all I had, and somehow I knew that He was all I needed. I knew that no matter what happened to my family, God would never leave nor forsake me, and through the Holy Spirit, God was always with me and always available to me.

God made it clear to me that He did not create me to be a math teacher and/or a basketball coach. Those are great endeavors and can make a huge difference in this world, but it was not what God had created, equipped, and called me to do. He made it clear to me that summer that He was not joking when He told me to go into vocational ministry in ninth grade. In order to be obedient to Him, I had to shift my focus and take the necessary steps to make it happen, not worry about what other people said about my decision to go into ministry.

I made many decisions that summer. I decided that I was going to quit the fraternity I was in because I couldn't be a part of it and pursue Jesus like I needed to. I decided I was going to be a basketball manager through my junior year, but after that I was going to move home and live at home with my dad while I student-taught during my senior year. I decided that I was going to pursue a Master of Divinity degree because being raised Southern Baptist, that's just what you did for going into ministry.

I finished my time at Clemson, and made the decision to pursue my Masters degree at Gardner-Webb University's School of Divinity.

The summer before I began Divinity School, I served as the summer youth intern at First Baptist Church in Shelby, North Carolina. I walked into their contemporary service my first Sunday on the job in the beginning of June 2007, and from all the way across the room, I spotted this girl in a beautiful dress with a really nice figure. I soon found out that she was single, she was the pastor's daughter, AND later she became my wife! Here's our story...

Chapter 2

Our Story

Erin and I met on that first Sunday in June, but I'm sorry to admit to you that because I was a little nervous, I didn't pay her much attention that day, and some might even say I ignored her.

We ended up hanging out a few times, and one Wednesday night when Erin was sick, she skipped choir practice. She asked me if I wanted to go get some ice cream with her and a few other people from the church. I went, and everyone else bailed on us, so it ended up being just the two of us getting ice cream at Dairy Queen.

We talked for several hours that night, to the point where her dad texted her and asked, "How much ice cream does it take to make your throat feel better?" We went out the next Friday night to Ruby Tuesdays and to see a movie, and after that it was clear to me that she could be the woman I would marry.

A couple of weeks later, I was on a mission trip with the church youth group. One morning I was sitting at breakfast drinking coffee beside Erin's dad. I decided I was going to be very chivalrous, so I asked her dad if he would be ok with Erin and me officially dating. He looked at me and said, "That's her decision." So, after the mission trip ended, we began dating. We were engaged 11 months later, and a year after that on May 23, 2009, we were married.

Our first year of marriage was interesting, as we were figuring out how to balance school, my youth pastor work, and living in the same town as her parents. I brought a lot of baggage into our marriage because of what had happened to my parents. It was hard for me to trust Erin, and it was easy for me to assume that she would do the same thing to me that my mom had done to my dad. She was constantly saying, "I'm not your mom, and you're not your dad."

During our second year of marriage, we knew God was calling us to move to Spartanburg, SC, so we stepped out in faith with no jobs, no friends, and no family. I did some substitute teaching, Erin had a job at a fitness center, and we loved Spartanburg. In partnership with being on staff as the Guest Services/First Impressions pastor at Milestones Church, I eventually ended up going on staff with Fellowship of Christian Athletes as the chaplain at USC Upstate.

In 2011, we felt God call us to step away from there and be part of NewSpring Church. I ended up being hired at NewSpring on January 1, 2012, as the Volunteer Director at the Spartanburg Campus. Later that year, I was given the opportunity to move to Greenwood, SC and launch a campus there as the Campus Pastor.

I'm not sure when my workaholism began. I grew up with a dad who was very tough on me because that's how he was raised, and also because he knew how great I could be. He was tough on me in school, he was tough on me on the field or the court, and he was even tough on me when I cut grass. He always demanded the best out of me, and he had high expectations. When I cut grass, I either took too long, or I missed some, or I used too much gas. When I played basketball, missing free throws or layups was unacceptable. When I was on the mound, he expected a very favorable strike/ball ratio. In school, I was expected to make 100's, not just A's.

This helped me to excel in school and sports, and really, in anything that I did. It helped me to develop a work ethic that has set me apart from some of my peers. However, it also gave the Enemy a foothold to plant some lies in my mind.

It allowed him to plant the lie I started to believe that went a little something like, "Nothing you do will ever be good enough, and your value is measured by your performance." This created an obsessive need and desire to prove myself, to strive to please people in order to prove I was good enough and that I was valuable.

I became a workaholic. I had an affair with my job. I worked tirelessly, putting the church and the needs of other people ahead of the needs of my wife. I always knew that being married in ministry was going to be tough because Paul says this in his first letter to the church at Corinth:

> *I want you to be without concerns. The unmarried man is concerned about the things of the Lord—how he may please the Lord. But the married man is concerned about the things of the world—how he may please his wife— and his interests are divided. The unmarried woman or virgin is concerned about the things of the Lord, so that she may be holy both in body and in spirit. But the married woman is concerned about the things of the world—how she may please her husband.*
>
> –1 Corinthians 7:32-24 (CSB)

Because I am a follower of Jesus Christ and, therefore, in ministry, and because I am also married, God calls me to steward both of those things well. This is difficult for anyone who is married and in ministry, because your interests are somewhat divided. You have to be concerned about the things of the Lord and about how you may please your spouse, but these things don't have to necessarily war against each other. I didn't balance these things very well, and I created a situation for my wife where she felt like I couldn't take care of her needs, and that she was burdening me by sharing anything with me because I was so busy tending to the needs, cares, concerns, and worries of other people.

While I was having an affair with my job, I found out on September 7, 2014 that my wife was having an affair with my former staff member. I was crushed and devastated and I could not believe that what happened to my mom and dad was now happening to me and my marriage. My worst fear and nightmare was coming true.

The very next Sunday we told our volunteers, and I was given four months off of work so Erin and I could work on our marriage and spend time in some intensive counseling. God has done so much, healed so much, grown us so much. Now our marriage is healthier than ever, and this book is a testament to that.

In the next several chapters, I will share with you the things that God has done and what He has taught us along the way, simply because we did it wrong and he allowed it to be fixed early in our lives. We are definitely not experts, we're just sharing our experience and bragging on God! However, before I get there, I want to share a couple of things God did for me personally through this trial.

In Beth Moore's book, "When Godly People do Ungodly Things", she talks about the story of Peter denying Jesus and being restored back into ministry in John 21. One of the things she shares is that in her opinion and understanding, Peter had to go through the process of denying Jesus and getting restored back into ministry so that the pride in his heart as a fisherman could be sifted out and removed in order for him to become the shepherd he needed to be for God to build His Church. I'm not sure if I *had to* go through this process in order for God to heal me and change my heart. Maybe God tried to get my attention in other ways and couldn't, but I do know that God definitely did use this to heal me and change my heart in several ways.

The first thing He did was to change my heart in the exact same way that He changed Peter's heart. I was operating as a "fisherman" in ministry in a lot of ways. I was concerned only with how many fish there were, how big the fish were, and if they weren't big enough, I didn't care enough about them to keep them. I was so concerned with "success" and with how I looked, and with what people could do to help "my ministry".

However, God transformed the heart of a "fisherman in ministry" to the heart of a shepherd so I could continue leading His Church. He gave me a heart that cared about each individual person. A heart that didn't care who they were, because they were all His sheep. A heart that cared for the hurting, and a heart that cared for little lambs, new sheep, and old sheep. He turned my heart into one of compassion, sympathy, and empathy, and because of this I have found greater joy in what God has called me to do.

He also used this to speak truth into some of the lies that I was believing. It was through reading the story of Jesus getting baptized after everything happened that I realized in that story, Jesus hadn't accomplished anything in ministry or anything for God at this point in His life. He had simply been a son, a student, and a carpenter; obedient, and faithful. God looked down on Jesus in that moment and said, "This is My beloved son, with whom I am well-pleased."

I realized that I am good enough, and not because of anything to do with me, but everything to do with the fact that I am a child of God, and my value is not wrapped up in my performance, but in my position as God's son. This truth set me free in so many ways, and I felt freedom knowing that I was loved by God, that He is pleased with me, and that I need to live for an audience of One and not to please or prove myself to anyone.

The third thing that God showed and taught me in this time is that marriage is not a hindrance or something that keeps you from being "successful". It is true that marriage might keep you from getting as much done. It is true that marriage might limit some of the things you say yes to, or the number of hours you work, or the amount of time you travel, or the amount of time that you have to work on projects, and if that is your definition of success, then marriage might keep you from becoming "successful".

However, I would like to pose to you that maybe that is not what success actually is all about. What if the reason you were put on this Earth, and what true success is, is becoming more like Jesus Christ, and becoming the person that God wants you to be? What if success has way more to do with the person that you are becoming and way less to do with the things you are accomplishing? While marriage might limit the things that you can do/accomplish, it has the ability to multiply the person that you are becoming, and make you more like Jesus if you let it!

The last thing the Lord did in me during this time was to help me realize a deep truth about His Church. Several times in Scripture, the Church (believers in Jesus, not a building) is called the Bride of Christ. It is never called the "bride of the pastor who leads a local context of the body of Christ." It is not *my* bride, it is not *my* church, it is God's Church, and it is the Bride of Christ, and He will take care of it! However, I am the only husband my wife will have, and the only father my kids will have. Anyone can do what I do in ministry, and God can replace me any day. However, no one will ever be able to replace the calling I have at home, and that needs to be my first priority!

I, along with many other Christians, had been taught for some portion of my life that being a follower of Jesus means we will be blessed. Your life will be better, you will not have as many negative things/circumstances happen to you, you will be blessed financially, etc. While some of those things might happen *for* you, it's not a guarantee.

I have learned that being a Christian *does* mean that you can live a blessed and abundant life full of hope, joy, and peace, but sometimes the way that God accomplishes those things in our lives is through our trials and difficulties. Many times those trials, tribulations, and difficulties are the things that God uses in our lives to accomplish His purposes and promises and to make us more like His Son.

I know that He doesn't promise an easy life, but in times of trial I can lean into the things that I know are true! Things like:

> *We know that all things work together for the good of those who love God, who are called according to His purpose.*
> –Romans 8:28 (CSB)

> *You will have suffering in this world. Be Courageous! I have conquered the world.*
> –John 16:33 (CSB)

> *A thief* [our enemy] *comes only to steal and kill and destroy. I* [Jesus] *have come so that they may have life and have it in abundance.*
> –John 10:10 (CSB)

While being a follower of Jesus doesn't mean that I will not face storms in life, it does mean that I have an anchor and a foundation to cling to in those storms, and that because of that, no matter my circumstances, I can have abundant life!

Chapter 3

Why Does Marriage Matter?

I think before we ever get to the place of putting marriage in the proper, God-honoring, biblical context, we have to answer these questions: Why does marriage even matter in the first place? Where did it begin? What are the purposes of marriage?

We live in a society where marriage has become more unimportant in our culture than ever before. People are living together without being married more than ever before. Studies suggest that around 75% of all adults under thirty have lived with someone before getting married. People are having more premarital sex than ever before in order to make sure that the relationship will "work". Studies tell us that only 3% of Americans wait until they are married to have sex. People are getting divorced at a higher clip than ever before. Studies show that 50% of all marriages in America end in divorce. That includes 41% of first marriages, 60% of second marriages, and 73% of third marriages.

A big part of this, in my opinion, is because of what we have turned marriage into. It has become something that isn't attractive to other people because of the way so many marriages are operating. We have so many married couples today that are simply living as roommates. There is no spiritual, physical, or emotional intimacy, and many people are simply sharing a space and the chores that come along with it.

Many marriages have become nothing more than business partnerships. They work, they drop off the kids and then pick them up, go to bed, and start all over again the next day. We have also turned sex inside of marriage into a boring business transaction because we selfishly need to be relieved.

On Amazon, there are 151,000 books on marriage, and the ads on the same page are promoting divorce lawyers. There are 190,000 books on sex on Amazon, and on that same page you'll find ads for addiction counselors. There are obviously lots of people who are looking for help and answers who haven't been able to find the help they are looking for. I think it's because we don't truly understand the meaning of marriage.

I think the reason marriage matters is to make us more like Jesus and to show other people the gospel. I think that if we really grasp onto this, then our marriages can truly thrive and not just survive. In order for our marriages to thrive and for them to show others the gospel as we become more like Jesus, we must embrace the fact that no marriage accidentally thrives. We will always drift towards survival and not towards thriving, so it is something that will take some intentional effort on our part.

There has never been an NFL team that said, "I don't think we need practice, perhaps we'll just show up for our games without practicing or intentionally preparing, and maybe we'll win the Super Bowl." There has never been an NBA team that has accidentally won the Larry O'Brien Trophy, and there has never been a college team that accidentally won a championship. It took Dabo Swinney and my Clemson Tigers years of building culture, recruiting well, coaching up, and working out in order to win their first football championship in 2017 since 1981. You don't accidentally win championships, and your marriage doesn't accidentally thrive. There is a story in 2 Samuel 11 that dives into this further:

> *In the spring when kings march out to war,*
> *David sent Joab with his officers and all of*

Israel. *They destroyed the Ammonites and besieged Rabbah, but David remained in Jerusalem. One evening David got up from his bed and strolled around on the roof of the palace. From the roof he saw a woman bathing—a very beautiful woman. So David sent someone to inquire about her, and he said, "Isn't this Bathsheba, daughter of Eliam, and wife of Uriah the Hethite?" David sent messengers to get her, and when she came to him, he slept with her. Now she had just been purifying herself from her uncleanness. Afterward, she returned home. The woman conceived and sent word to inform David: "I am pregnant." David sent orders to Joab: "Send me Uriah the Hethite." So Joab sent Uriah to David. When Uriah came to him, David asked how Joab and the troops were doing, and how the war was going. Then he said to Uriah, "Go down to your house and wash your feet." So Uriah left the palace, and a gift from the king followed him. But Uriah slept at the door of the palace with all of his master's servants; he did not go down to his house. When it was reported to David, "Uriah didn't go home," David questioned Uriah, "Haven't you just come from a journey? Why didn't you go home?" Uriah answered David, "The ark, Israel, and Judah are dwelling in tents, and my master Joab and his soldiers are camping in the open field. How can I enter my house to eat and drink and sleep with my wife? As surely as you live and by your life, I will not do this!" "Stay here today also,"*

David said to Uriah, "and tomorrow I will send you back." So Uriah stayed in Jerusalem that day and the next. Then David invited Uriah to eat and drink with him, and David got him drunk. He went out in the evening to lie down on his cot with his master's servants, but he did not go home. The next morning David wrote a letter to Joab and sent it with Uriah. In the letter he wrote: Put Uriah at the front of the fiercest fighting, then withdraw from him so that he is struck down and dies. When Joab was besieging the city, he put Uriah in the place where he knew the best enemy soldiers were. Then the men of the city came out and attacked Joab, and some of the men from David's soldiers fell in battle; Uriah the Hethite also died. Joab sent someone to report to David all the details of the battle. He commanded the messenger, "When you've finished telling the king all the details of the battle—if the king's anger gets stirred up and he asks you, 'Why did you get so close to the city to fight? Didn't you realize they would shoot from the top of the wall? At Thebez, who struck Abimelech son of Jerubbesheth? Didn't a woman drop an upper millstone on him from the top of the wall so that he died? Why did you get so close to the wall?'—then say, 'Your servant Uriah the Hethite is dead also.'" Then the messenger left. When he arrived, he reported to David all that Joab had sent him to tell. The messenger reported to David, "The men gained the advantage over us and came out against

*us in the field, but we counterattacked right
up to the entrance of the city gate. However,
the archers shot down on your servants from
the top of the wall, and some of the king's
servants died. Your servant Uriah the Hethite
is also dead." David told the messenger, "Say
this to Joab: 'Don't let this matter upset you
because the sword devours all alike. Intensify
your fight against the city and demolish it.'
Encourage him." When Uriah's wife heard that
her husband Uriah had died, she mourned for
him. When the time of mourning ended, David
had her brought to his house. She became his
wife and bore him a son. However, the Lord
considered what David had done to be evil.*

–2 Samuel 11:1-27 (CSB)

The thing that I notice about this passage of Scripture happens in the very first verse. It says that at the time when kings normally go out to war, David didn't go and wasn't intentional about doing what he was supposed to be doing, and instead sent someone to lead the troops in his place. His lack of intentionality created the environment where all of these other things fell into place. He put himself in a position where he was vulnerable to temptation, and he gave in, which led to adultery, an unwanted pregnancy, and the death of an adult and a child. I believe this is why it's so important to be intentional in our marriages. I have heard several people tell me that failing to plan is like planning to fail. We must be intentional, and we must be deliberate because our marriages will never accidentally thrive.

Since we know why marriage matters, and that we must be intentional with our marriages in order for them to thrive, we now move to the question of "Where did marriage come from in the first place, and why does it even exist?" In the very beginning of the Word of God, we see that God creates everything, and He declares everything good! One of the things that God creates in Genesis 1 is humans:

> *Then God said, Let us make man in our image, according to our likeness. They will rule the fish of the sea, the birds of the sky, the livestock, the whole earth, and the creatures that crawl on the earth." So God created man in his own image; he created him in the image of God; he created them male and female. God blessed them, and God said to them, "Be fruitful, multiply, fill the earth, and subdue it. Rule the fish of the sea, the birds of the sky, and every creature that crawls on the earth.*
>
> –Genesis 1:26-28 (CSB)

God created man with all the desires, anatomy, and hormones, and according to the Bible, before sin entered the world it is good! We then see in Chapter 2, that even though it was good, there was still one issue that needed to be figured out. It never takes long when there are only men around for some kind of issue to spring up.

> *These are the records of the heavens and the earth, concerning their creation. At the time that the Lord God made the earth and the heavens, no shrub of the field had yet grown on the land, and no plant of the field had yet sprouted, for the Lord God had not made it rain on the land, and there was no man to*

work the ground. But mist would come up from the earth and water all the ground. Then the Lord God formed the man out of the dust from the ground and breathed the breath of life into his nostrils, and the man became a living being. The Lord God planted a garden in Eden, in the east, and there he placed the man he had formed. The Lord God caused to grow out of the ground every tree pleasing in appearance and good for food, including the tree of life in the middle of the garden, as well as the tree of the knowledge of good and evil. A river went out from Eden to water the garden. From there it divided and became the source of four rivers. The name of the first is Pishon, which flows through the entire land of Havilah, where there is gold. Gold from that land is pure; bdellium and onyx are also there. The name of the second river is Gihon, which flows through the entire land of Cush. The name of the third river is Tigris, which runs east of Assyria. And the fourth river is the Euphrates. The Lord God took the man and placed him in the garden of Eden to work it and watch over it. And the Lord God commanded the man, "You are free to eat from any tree of the garden, but you must not eat from the tree of the knowledge of good and evil, for on the day you eat from it, you will certainly die." Then the Lord God said, "It is not good for the man to be alone. I will make a helper corresponding to him." The Lord God formed out of the ground every wild animal and every bird of the sky, and brought each

to the man to see what he would call it. And whatever the man called a living creature, that was its name. The man gave names to all the livestock, to the birds of the sky, and to every wild animal; but for the man no helper was found corresponding to him. So the Lord God caused a deep sleep to come over the man, and he slept. God took one of his ribs and closed the flesh at that place. Then the Lord God made the rib he had taken from the man into a woman and brought her to the man. And the man said, "This one, at last, is bone of my bone, and flesh of my flesh; this one will be called 'woman,' for she was taken from man." This is why a man leaves his father and mother and bonds with his wife, and they become one flesh. Both the man and his wife were naked, yet felt no shame.
                                    –Genesis 2:4-25 (CSB)

God created Adam and it was good, however, it didn't take long for Adam and God to realize that man needed a helper (always have and always will). If you don't believe that men need a helpmate then just get to know a single male and spend a few days with him, and it will become very clear, very quickly why the Bible says that man needed a helper.

God created Adam a helper and named her Eve. She was taken out of Adam, compatible for Adam, and was created very differently and unique from Adam, but also very similar to him. She was created *for* Adam! God created them, brought them together, and saw that it was good. It says that man and wife are supposed to put their relationship ahead of other earthly relationships, bond with each other and cling to each other to become one flesh.

I think this clearly shows us that marriage is to be considered the most important earthly relationship that we have, and I believe it shows us that it is to be a relationship that does not end. Two can become one, but one cannot separate back into two without a lot of pain and trouble and heartache. I believe this is why we must remember that God created marriage to be a covenant and not a contract.

A contract is where both parties have some responsibility, where there are rights given to both parties, but there is always an exit clause. If one party doesn't uphold their end of the contract, or if one party just wants a way out because they want a change or something different, there is always a way out. You might have to pay some kind of penalty, but you can always get out of it.

A contract is a very conditional thing based on actions, feelings, and circumstances. There are so many people today who treat marriage this way. They treat marriage as if it's not a big deal, just a simple contract that if their spouse doesn't uphold their end of the bargain, or if they just decide they want out one day, it's perfectly fine.

We treat marriage as a very conditional thing, and depending on the actions, feelings, or circumstances, we are fine with changing our marital status. There are so many people today who get married because in the back of their mind they can always get out. There are so many people who say the words "til death do us part," and "I will be with you for richer or poorer, in sickness and in health," but they don't actually mean those words, and instead mean, "until I feel like parting," "as long as we are financially stable, I'll stay," or "as long as we are healthy, I'll stay." The moment their feelings or circumstances change, the moment financial trouble hits, or the moment that sickness hits, they push the eject button.

I believe that God has always intended for marriage to be a covenant. I think God wants our marriages to mirror the covenant He has made to His Church, His people. A covenant is unconditional, and there is no exit clause. A covenant gives both parties responsibilities and rights, however, there is no way out.

When you enter into a covenant, you are saying I am in this thing no matter what. I don't care if feelings change, circumstances change, if actions change, I am not going anywhere. This is what God does for us! I think this is why God calls us His bride! He wants us to know that no matter what, He will always be there, He will always love us, and no matter what, He will never leave us nor forsake us. If we have placed our faith in Jesus, there is nothing that we can do to escape or separate ourselves from the grace and love of God. I believe this is the way that God wants us to see our marriages.

In the original Greek language of the New Testament, we find four different words for love. We have diluted all of these into one English word, love, and the meaning is subjective based on who is using it. However, in the time of Jesus this wasn't the case. The four words are:

- **Phileo**—this would have been the word they used to describe the love between two friends. It's brotherly love, love for your co-worker, acquaintances, etc.
- **Storge**—this would have been the word used to describe the love parents have for their children, and the love children have for their parents.
- **Eros**—this would have been the word used to describe a sexual, lustful type of love for someone.
- **Agape**—this would have been the word used for the love between a man and his wife, and the love God has for us.

I think it's interesting that the same word used for love between a man and wife is the exact same word that's used for the love that God has for His children. I believe that it's no coincidence, because God wants us to love our spouse with the same covenantal love that He loves us with. God has always intended for our marriages to be seen as covenants and not contracts, so when did everything go wrong?

After God created Adam and Eve and they become one and are naked, feeling no shame or guilt, and everything is good and perfect and just as it's intended to be, we are introduced to our next character in the creation story:

> Now the serpent was the most cunning of all the wild animals that the Lord God had made. He said to the woman, "Did God really say, 'You can't eat from any tree in the garden?'" The woman said to the serpent, "We may eat the fruit from the trees in the garden. But about the fruit of the tree in the middle of the garden, God said, 'You must not eat it or touch it, or you will die.'" "No! You will not die," the serpent said to the woman. "In fact, God knows that when you eat it your eyes will be opened and you will be like God, knowing good and evil." The woman saw that the tree was good for food and delightful to look at, and that it was desirable for obtaining wisdom. So she took some of its fruit and ate it; she also gave some to her husband, who was with her, and he ate it. Then the eyes of both of them were opened, and they knew they were naked; so they sewed fig leaves together and made coverings for themselves. Then the man and his wife heard the sound

of the Lord God walking in the garden at the time of the evening breeze, and they hid from the Lord God among the trees of the garden. So the Lord God called out to the man and said to him, "Where are you?" And he said, "I heard you in the garden, and I was afraid because I was naked, so I hid." Then he asked, "Who told you that you were naked? Did you eat from the tree that I commanded you not to eat from?" The man replied, "The woman you gave to be with me—she gave me some fruit from the tree, and I ate." So the Lord God asked the woman, "What is this you have done?" And the woman said, "The serpent deceived me, and I ate." So the Lord God said to the serpent, "Because you have done this, you are cursed more than any livestock and more than any wild animal. You will move on your belly and eat dust all the days of your life. I will put hostility between you and the woman, and between your offspring and her offspring. He will strike your head, and you will strike his heel." He said to the woman, "I will intensify your labor pains; you will bear children with painful effort. Your desire will be for your husband, yet he will rule over you." And he said to the man, "Because you listened to your wife and ate from the tree about which I commanded you, 'Do not eat from it,' the ground is cursed because of you. You will eat from it by means of painful labor all the days of your life. It will produce thorns and thistles for you, and you will eat the plants of the field. You will eat bread by the sweat of your brow

until you return to the ground, since you were
taken from it. For you are dust, and you will
return to dust." The man named his wife Eve
because She was the mother of all the living.
The Lord God made clothing from skins for the
man and his wife, and he clothed them. The
Lord God said, "Since the man has become like
one of us, knowing good and evil, he must not
reach out, take from the tree of life, eat, and
live forever." So the Lord God sent him away
from the garden of Eden to work the ground
from which he was taken. He drove the man out
and stationed the cherubim and the flaming,
whirling sword east of the garden of Eden to
guard the way to the tree of life.

–Genesis 3:1-24 (CSB)

This is where we begin to see when marriage became so difficult. We see Adam and Eve's relationship with God and each other get fractured. Everything that was created good became able to be used as something potentially bad. There are some misconceptions in this Scripture that we hear taught from time to time, that aren't in the text.

Here are the things we do know. We know God told Adam that he could eat absolutely anything he laid his eyes on except for the one tree in the middle of the garden, the tree of the knowledge of good and evil. If he did, he would die. I do believe that God meant that they would no longer be eternal beings if they ate from this tree, but I also believe that He meant that they would die emotionally and spiritually as well. We do know that Adam passed along the message to Eve, because when the serpent comes to her and asked her if God really said that, she confirms His statement.

The serpent then gets crafty and tries to make Eve believe that God lied to her and is holding out on her, and that if she will simply eat of that tree she will receive what every human has wanted since the beginning of time: to be like God. It's the thing that got Satan kicked out of heaven, and it's the thing that humans still struggle with today. Eve listens to the serpent, sees the fruit and can't resist it, so she disobeys God and eats it anyway.

The Bible tells us that she then gave some to Adam, who was with her, and he ate it as well. We don't know that Adam was with Eve while the serpent was talking to her, but we do know that he was with her when she ate the fruit. Adam is the one God gave the message to in the first place, and He gave Adam the responsibility of leading and caring for his wife.

Instead of leading her and keeping her from disobeying God, Adam sits by apathetically and lets her eat the fruit, and then disobeys God and eats the fruit himself. In this part of the passage, we see our tendency as humans to want to be God, to want to know everything, to want to be in control, and our tendency to be apathetic towards each other and how dangerous those things can be.

Once they disobey God in this way, everything changes. Their eyes are opened to their nakedness, and they start feeling guilt and shame for the first time and try to cover themselves up. This is what we try to do today as well. We feel guilt and shame, our eyes are opened, and our first response is to try to fix it ourselves and to cover ourselves up, but we soon see how inadequate that is. They knew they had done wrong, and so when God shows up, they both try to hide from God because they are afraid of what He will say and do. Hiding from the One who created hide-and-seek, and is the best hide-and-seek player that there will ever be, is not a very smart idea. You would think that after eating from the forbidden tree they would have come up with something a little bit better.

God finds them and asks them if they disobeyed Him, and that's when the blame game started. Adam blamed Eve and God, because God was the one that created Eve, and Eve was the one that gave Adam the fruit. Eve blames the serpent because he is the one that deceived her. We still play the blame-game in our marriages today. We are victims and nothing is ever our fault. It's always our spouse's fault, or someone else's fault, or "the devil made me do it."

We then see God hand down consequences to the serpent, the man, and the woman, because disobeying God always has consequences. The consequences were that marriage, life, childbirth, and working would be extremely difficult from that point forward. It also included them being moved from God's perfect garden, Eden, to live in an imperfect world, that because of sin has always been and will always be rebelling against God.

But because God is so loving and loves us with agape love, He doesn't just leave them to do this on their own with the coverings that they made for themselves. God made clothing for them so that they could be covered. He made this clothing from lambskins, foreshadowing the covering He would send for us when He sent His son Jesus to die on the cross for our sins, and then resurrected Him from the dead to prove that sin and death had been defeated forever.

As humans, we have always and will always try to do things for ourselves. However, it is simply impossible to repair, re-establish, and put back together our relationship with God without the covering that God has provided for us in Jesus Christ!

We have now answered why marriage matters and where marriage came from, and will end this chapter by answering the question of what the purpose of marriage is. I think there are many purposes of marriage, however, I think there are four big categories we can talk about that encompass most of them.

The first purpose of marriage is intimacy. When we think of intimacy, we automatically think of sex, but God's definition of intimacy is so much bigger than that. It does include physical intimacy, but, it also includes spiritual intimacy, emotional intimacy, and mental intimacy. It is our souls being mended together. It is oneness, transparency, vulnerability, and living with no fear of rejection or humiliation from our spouse. It is two becoming one, and us being naked together and feeling no shame.

The second purpose of marriage is children. Procreation is a huge part of marriage—after all, God told us to be fruitful and multiply. One of the greatest joys and responsibilities in marriage is to have children and to raise them to be men and women of God!

The third purpose of marriage is companionship. Adam had a need for a helper that was compatible to him, so God gave him Eve as a gift; a helper. Companionship is a huge part of marriage. One of the biggest parts in having a marriage that succeeds is to be friends! I believe that God designed us to put our relationship with Him first, our relationship and friendship with our spouse second, and everything else below that!

The last and most important purpose in marriage is to bring glory to God! The universal purpose of every life and every marriage is to bring glory to God in everything that we do. We are created to serve, to make an impact, and to bring glory to God through that.

Marriage is a gift that refines us, and makes us more like Jesus, so that we can live lives that make a difference and bring glory to God! I believe that Gary Thomas is right when he tells us that God created and intended marriage to be much more about our holiness than our happiness. God has given us marriage to help us fulfill our earthly purpose of giving glory to God and being made into the image of His Son!

Marriage is a little like a photograph or a mirror. Have you ever had a picture taken, and then when you saw the picture, you were a little disgusted by what you saw? Just the other day, my wife showed me a picture that we took as a family at the beach, and I wasn't excited about the way I looked, so I decided something needed to be done about it.

When we look in the mirror, we might notice something that we think we need to take action on. Maybe it's us noticing we need to lose some weight, or maybe it's us realizing we need to take care of the booger we found in our nose. Marriage can do that same thing for us. It can show us the places where we are falling short of being like Jesus, and can help us to know what to do in order to become more like Him!

Many times in marriage, the key is endurance and perseverance. God kept the Israelites in the desert for 40 years before allowing them to go into the promised land because they needed to be refined. They had to persevere and endure the desert for 40 years in order to become who God wanted them to become before they could enter the promised land. Here is what the book of James says:

> Consider it a great joy, my brothers and sisters, whenever you experience various trials, because you know that the testing of your faith produces endurance. And let endurance have its full effect, so that you may be mature and complete, lacking nothing. Blessed is the one who endures trials, because when he has stood the test he will receive the crown of life that God has promised to those who love him.
> –James 1:2-3, 12 (CSB)

He tells us that many times we go through trials in order to test our faith, and these trials produce endurance. Endurance, if we don't give up, produces spiritual maturity. It allows us to face trials and become more like Jesus! The word used for testing and trials in these verses is the same Greek word used for the refining of silver.

In case you are like me and don't refine silver on a daily basis, let me take you through the process. They take a big blob of unrefined silver and put it in a massive pot. They heat it up to an incredibly high temperature, and the impurities of the silver rise to the top. This is called the dross, and they scrape it off the top once it gets there. They then heat it up again, and when the impurities rise to the top, they scrape off the dross again. This process continues to repeat itself over and over until the maker and refiner of the silver can look down into the silver and see his image reflected in it.

This same thing happens to us when we go through trials. The heat is turned up in our lives so that the impurities can make their way to the surface to be dealt with, so that eventually, God can look down and see the image of His Son reflected in us. This is why marriage is so important. It helps us become more like Jesus, and while it might keep us from accomplishing certain things, it can definitely multiply who we become as our aim in this world is to become more like Jesus!

We have answered the questions of why marriage matters, where marriage came from, and what are the purposes of marriage. Next we turn our attention to some practical marriage advice, starting with the roles of a husband and wife in marriage.

- **What do you need to be more intentional about in your marriage and in your life?**
- **Do you see marriage more as a contract or a covenant?**
- **What are the purposes of marriage?**
- **What needs to be refined in you?**

Chapter 4

Roles and Responsibilities

I really do believe that marriage is the best way to show the gospel of Jesus Christ to people. Marriage is the most important human relationship we have, and if it is done correctly, it can show other people the way God interacts in relationship with us. We will begin talking about some practical things that we can do in our marriages to help them thrive, and we are going to begin with what I think is one of the most important things in all of marriage.

We must figure out what our spouse needs if we ever want to be successful in our marriages. We have to know our roles! I don't mean that we have to sit down with a list of chores and figure out what the husband is going to do and what the wife is going to do, although that may help you. What I mean when I say "know your role" is that we must know what a man's role in a biblical marriage is and what a woman's role in a biblical marriage is.

Looking at it from a broad view, you can really summarize it as so many people have in this way: women need to be loved and cared for, and a man's role is to give her that love. Men need respect and trust, and a woman's role is to give him that respect and trust. However, I don't want to just look at it broadly, I want to dig a little deeper, and we're going to do that by looking at a passage of Scripture that I think best tells us how a marriage should work. It's a passage that comes out of the Apostle Paul's letter to the church of Ephesus as he is instructing them on how all of the major relationships in our lives should work. Here is what he says about the marriage relationship:

> *Wives, submit to your husbands as to the Lord, because the husband is the head of the wife as Christ is the head of the church. He is the Savior of the body. Now as the church submits to Christ, so also wives are to submit to their husbands in everything. Husbands, love your wives, just as Christ loved the church and gave himself for her to make her holy, cleansing her with the washing of water by the word. He did this to present the church to himself in splendor, without spot or wrinkle or anything like that, but holy and blameless. In the same way, husbands are to love their wives as their own bodies. He who loves his wife loves himself. For no one ever hates his own flesh but provides and cares for it, just as Christ does for the church, since we are members of his body. **For this reason a man will leave his father and mother and be joined to his wife, and the two will become one flesh** [emphasis added]. This mystery is profound, but I am talking about Christ and the church. To sum up, each one of you is to love his wife as himself, and the wife is to respect her husband.*
>
> –Ephesians 5:22-33 (CSB)

This passage of Scripture has gotten some bad press recently, because people in our culture and society in today's day and age hate the word "submit" due to how that word's connotation has changed. It does say for wives to submit to their husbands, but most people leave out the rest of this sentence, which says, "Submit to them as to the Lord." That means that the reason the wife is to submit to her husband is not because he can rule over her, enslave her, or tell her what to do and therefore she has to do it, but because Jesus has placed man as the head of the house, as the one who will be responsible for the spiritual well-being of the household, and the wife is to trust and submit to her husband because she trusts and submits to Jesus Christ.

In my opinion, I believe that this submission is based on having a husband that is exhibiting the same characteristics in the marriage relationship as Christ does towards us as His people.

Paul then moves on to tell us that it is the responsibility of the husband to love his wife just as Christ loved the church and gave himself for her. In other words, husbands are to love their wives by sacrificing for them, giving up their rights for them, putting their needs, wants, and desires over their own, and being willing to serve and sacrifice for them even to the point of dying for them. Husbands are also to help their wives become more like Jesus, and the way they are to do that is to make sure that Scripture is a massive part of the household and their routine. He then goes back to talking about loving our wives in the same way that we love ourselves.

The fact is that if most husbands would love their wives as much as they love themselves, marriages would be in a different place. We live in a society where husbands put themselves over everyone and everything else, and if we would simply be willing to love our wives in that way, I believe it would change so much.

We love ourselves by providing and caring for ourselves, and husbands are supposed to provide and care for their wives in that same way. I don't think it is a coincidence that Paul spends way more time addressing the husbands than he does the wives. He expects a lot out of husbands because it is a huge responsibility.

The last part of this passage quotes what we talked about earlier out of the book of Genesis, and it says that husbands and wives are to join together and become one flesh, mingled together, fully transparent, honest, vulnerable, and becoming one. He ends by summarizing everything, and it is what so many books have written about—which shouldn't be any surprise to us, because men and women needed the same thing 2,000 years ago as they do now. Women need love, and it is man's responsibility to give that to them, and men need respect, and it is the woman's responsibility to give that to him.

That's what the Bible tells us the role of a man and woman inside of marriage is, but now I want to look at some other practical things that we can do in order to fulfill the roles that God has given us. Since Paul spends more time addressing men and their role and responsibility, let's start with them first.

A man's major responsibility in marriage according to Ephesians 5 is to love his wife—specifically, to love his wife as Christ loved the Church; He gave Himself up for her—and to love his wife as he loves himself. He must love his wife by constantly sacrificing, humbling himself, and dying to himself on a daily basis. In other words, he must make everything about his spouse and her needs, wants, and desires! Here are 5 practical things a man can do in order to love his wife well:

- **Love Jesus well and pray for her.** The best thing a man can do to love his wife well is to follow Jesus and lead her into doing the same thing. He must be someone who leads the family spiritually by reading his Bible, leading the family in prayer, and making sure that his family is plugged into a local community of faith and a smaller community of believers that are sharpening each other.

One of the greatest things you can do for your wife is to pray for her on a daily basis.

- **Being present.** We were created to work—as Adam was told to work before sin ever entered the world—and it was good. Sin might have made work more difficult, but we were created to work, and we must work and work hard. You will never achieve a 50/50 work/life balance, but you can always be 100% present wherever you are. When you are at work, be 100% present at work so that you can be as efficient and time conscious as possible, that way when you get home you can be 100% present at home. This is honestly a great way to live life, no matter where you are. If you are with friends be 100% present, if you are at church be 100% present, if you are at a meal or work lunch be 100% present. Let's make it our goal to not complain about how much time we do or don't have in certain instances, but to be fully engaged, no matter how much time we have!

- **Date her.** There are way too many marriages where the wedding day signaled the end of dating. One of the great things a man can do to love his wife well is to continue dating her after they are married. Pursue her, ask her on dates, plan the date and what to do and talk about. We must make this a priority! Don't fall into the trap before having kids of thinking that every night is date night. Have an intentional, weekly date night every week, no matter what stage your marriage is in. You might have to get creative to make it happen. It might have to happen on the back porch after you put your kids to sleep, but it can happen on a regular basis, if you are intentional!

- **Help her.** Your wife is not your mom, and she is not your maid, so help her around the house. Pitch in and take some things off of her plate. Ask her what are one or two things that she hates doing the most, and continually do those things so she doesn't have to. Sit down with her and ask her if she feels pressured to get housework done, and ask her how you can help take some of that pressure off of her.

- **Protect her.** Your wife must feel safe physically, emotionally, mentally, and financially, and it is your job to help make that happen. I think that we can do this by being a gardener and a guardian.

A gardener is someone who is willing to do whatever it takes to help their wife grow in their relationship with Jesus and remove anything that might keep her from growing. A gardener prepares the soil, plants the seeds, waters the seeds, weeds the garden, and keeps bugs and animals out.

A guardian is someone who guards or protects their wife. I don't think it's a coincidence that Eve was made out of Adam's rib. I think it was intentional because the job of a rib is to protect important organs, and Adam's job was to protect Eve because she was important. She was taken not from Adam's head to top him, or from his feet to be trampled on by him, but from his side to be equal with him, under his arm to be protected by him, and near his heart to be loved by him.

Let's now move to a woman's role and responsibility in marriage. According to Ephesians 5, the major responsibility of a woman in marriage is to respect her husband by submitting to him. If the man does the five things listed above, I believe his wife will have no problem respecting him!

However, what if he doesn't do those five things? What are you supposed to do then? If you know that he doesn't do those things before you are married, DON'T GET MARRIED! If you are already married, then the best thing for you to do is to pray for him constantly, and to be an example for him by reading your Bible and praying in places where he can see you. The reason for this is not to simply put your faith on show or show off, and not to try to prove you are "holier than thou" or doing it only because they are watching. The point is that your entire life needs to be lived for God, through Christ, and therefore your life will be an example to your spouse. You should do the things that Jesus asks us to do, but not be afraid to do those things in public in front of your spouse because you never know when it might make a difference.

When God makes Eve from Adam's rib, he does so because Adam needs a helper. I find it interesting that the other person in Scripture—outside of a wife—that we see called a helper, is the Holy Spirit. I don't think that it is the wife's responsibility to be the Holy Spirit for her husband, but I do think that wives do some of the same things for their husbands that the Holy Spirit does for believers. He helps us, he guides us, he teaches us, he strengthens us, and our wives do a lot of those same things.

Scripture also tells us that Eve is made from the rib of Adam, and in pottery, a rib helps to mold and shape the piece of pottery. I believe that part of the role of a wife is to help mold and shape her husband to become more like Jesus! Here are five things a wife can do to practically show respect to her husband:

- **Love Jesus well and pray for him.** The best thing a woman can do to love her husband well is to follow Jesus personally every single day and spend time praying for her husband.
- **Trust him.** One of the biggest things that a husband needs is a wife who trusts him. When you know that your wife trusts you, it feels like there is nothing impossible for you. We are all humans, so the reality is that we will mess up. We are all sinful in our flesh, so we cannot necessarily trust in the flesh of any human, including our spouse. However, as you see him loving Jesus and following Jesus, you can

trust Jesus inside of your husband, and you can trust your husband because of that!

- **Advise him.** One of the best things that the Holy Spirit does for a believer, and one of the best things a wife can do for her husband, is to give him advice! When he is in the process of making any kind of decision or questioning something, make sure that you clearly and calmly communicate to him your feelings and concerns. Give him good, solid, biblical advice, and after you have done these things, then hopefully you can...

- **Submit to him.** You have clearly communicated things to him, you have given him biblical advice, and you have prayed for him. Now, I hope that you are in a place that you can submit to him. Because of Jesus in Him, you can trust in and support the decisions that he makes, and he can feel empowered!

- **Encourage and Support him.** One of the things that every man needs, probably because we are insecure, is encouragement all the time! A wife should be her husband's biggest fan, biggest cheerleader, and be an encouragement to her husband with words and actions. One of the best things a wife can do for her husband is to encourage him by pursuing him and receiving his pursuit of her! Most of us men, just like Adam, can't do this life on our own. We need a spouse who can support us. We need a spouse who can help us where we are weak, and a spouse who is willing to serve and support the things that their husband is doing. This support can come from helping with things from work, helping with things at home, or maybe most importantly, it can come from praying for him on a daily basis!

I hope that you have a better idea of the biblical roles of a husband and wife, and some practical things you can do to fulfill those roles and responsibilities. I will end this chapter the same way that Paul ends his discussion of the roles and responsibilities of husbands and wives in his letter to the Ephesian church:

> *To sum up, each one of you is to love his wife as himself, and the wife is to respect her husband.*
> –Ephesians 5:33 (CSB)

- **What are the husband's and wife's roles in marriage?**
- **How can a husband love his wife well?**
- **How can a wife respect her husband well?**

Chapter 5

Secret to Contentment

Have you ever been in a situation where you thought, if I could just have this one thing it will make me content? Have you ever said, "I would be happy if I could just have that house, or that car, or that job, or that wife?" Did you ever say, "If I could just get married, then I will be content and fulfilled?"

I believe one of the most common misconceptions about marriage today is that it will fulfill us and make us content. We believe our spouse will fill the holes that are missing, and that marriage is the secret to being completely fulfilled and content. Then, we get married and realize that it didn't make us completely fulfilled. We realize that marriage isn't the secret to contentment. So, where do we go from here? What is the secret to contentment?

I believe the reason so many people aren't content and fulfilled in their lives today is because we are trying to fill the infinite holes in our lives with finite things. We are trying to fill holes that only the Creator can fill, with created things. We are living for Earth, but were created for heaven. We must realize that contentment is not about our marriage, our relationships, our job, our possessions or our circumstances, but about our relationship with the God of the Universe through Jesus Christ.

This is not a new struggle, but one in which mankind has been struggling with since the beginning. Adam and Eve ate the fruit because they thought it could give them something that they had been convinced was missing in their lives. In the story of Jacob and Esau in the book of Genesis, we see a young man, Esau, give up his long-term birthright, money, inheritance, land, and possessions for an earthly bowl of stew because he was more concerned about his short-term hunger rather than his long-term destiny.

We see Solomon—who is described up to that point in his life as the wisest and richest man to have ever lived—chase fulfillment and contentment his entire life. He realizes something is missing and tries to fill it with money, alcohol, women, and work, and comes to the conclusion that nothing under the sun, except for a relationship with God, actually fulfills us.

You can read about this in the book of Ecclesiastes, which Solomon wrote, in order to show how worthless and futile it was to try to fill your infinite soul with finite things. The Apostle Paul is someone who got it. He understood the secret to fulfillment and contentment. Here is what he writes in Philippians 4:

> *I rejoiced in the Lord greatly because once again you renewed your care for me. You were, in fact, concerned about me but lacked the opportunity to show it. I don't say this out of need, for I have learned to be content in whatever circumstances I find myself. I know both how to make do with little, and I know how to make do with a lot. In any and all circumstances I have learned the secret of being content—whether well fed or hungry, whether in abundance or in need. I am able to do all things through him who strengthens me.*
> –Philippians 4:10-13 (CSB)

The amazing thing about this passage of Scripture for me is that Paul penned these words while he was sitting in a prison cell. Paul knew that no matter what he had or what his circumstances were in life, the secret to contentment lies in our relationship with Jesus and the fact that He can fulfill us and that we can do all things through Him who strengthens us. Paul is telling us that nothing on earth can fulfill you, and if you realize the true secret of contentment, you can be content in even the most dire of circumstances. That's great news! We can always have joy, hope, and peace, no matter what's going on in our lives because of our relationship with Jesus!

This is the reason why I believe the secret to contentment inside of our marriage is to simply have our relationships correctly prioritized. If we put our relationship with God through Jesus first, and our relationship with our spouse second, and everything else after that, we can be fulfilled and content in our marriages! If we get these out of order at all, then we are setting ourselves up for failure.

If you put your spouse first and God after them, you will not be fulfilled. If you put work or sports or kids before God or before your spouse, you will not be fulfilled. This shouldn't be a surprise to us, because Jesus told us that the greatest commandment was to love God first, and the second one was to love others. This same equation applies to our marriages. Love God first, love your spouse second.

I struggled for a long time with not being fulfilled and content in my marriage. The issue for me has never been my relationship with God. I have always put my relationship with God first. I have never had a problem reading my Bible and praying on a daily basis, going to church, tithing, being in a small group, etc. My problem was what I put in the second position. My priority list was not God, then my spouse. My priority list was God, my job, success, meeting the needs and expectations of others, and then my wife. Every source of conflict, and lack of contentment and fulfillment in my marriage I can directly point back to a lack of priorities.

I read a book by Justin and Trisha Davis called "Beyond Ordinary: When a Good Marriage Just Isn't Good Enough", and they talked about the Messiah Complex and the Reverse Messiah Complex, and these are the things that Erin and I struggled with for the first several years of our marriage.

I struggled with the Messiah complex with Erin and others, thinking that I could be the savior, I could meet all the needs, I could fix anything. Erin struggled with the reverse Messiah complex which meant she was relying on me to fulfill her and help her be content. She was placing expectations on me that only Jesus could fulfill and was placing me on a pedestal, and because of my humanity, I was always going to fail to live up to those expectations. A lot of the expectations that she had for me were unrealistic and unspoken. Anytime we put our spouse in this position we are putting them in a position that they were never meant to be put in, and because of the weight and pressure which humans can't carry, they will always fail. This is why I believe that the biggest issue when it comes to contentment and fulfillment in our marriages is source confusion. We become confused with who or what our source should be. We try to make our spouse our source, or our jobs our source, or our kids our source, or sports our source, or crossfit our source, or ourselves our source and we must realize that contentment will never come this way.

There was a woman that Jesus had a conversation with one time that was struggling with source confusion. Here is how the story unfolded:

> When Jesus learned that the Pharisees had heard he was making and baptizing more disciples than John (though Jesus himself was

not baptizing, but his disciples were), he left Judea and went again to Galilee. He had to travel through Samaria; so he came to a town of Samaria called Sychar near the property that Jacob had given his son Joseph. Jacob's well was there, and Jesus, worn out from his journey, sat down at the well. It was about noon. A woman of Samaria came to draw water. "Give me a drink," Jesus said to her, because his disciples had gone into town to buy food. "How is it that you, a Jew, ask for a drink from me, a Samaritan woman?" she asked him. For Jews do not associate with Samaritans. Jesus answered, "If you knew the gift of God, and who is saying to you, 'Give me a drink,' you would ask him, and he would give you living water." "Sir," said the woman, "you don't even have a bucket, and the well is deep. So where do you get this 'living water'? You aren't greater than our father Jacob, are you? He gave us the well and drank from it himself, as did his sons and livestock." Jesus said, "Everyone who drinks from this water will get thirsty again. But whoever drinks from the water that I will give him will never get thirsty again. In fact, the water I will give him will become a well of water springing up in him for eternal life." "Sir," the woman said to him, "give me this water so that I won't get thirsty and come here to draw water." "Go call your husband," he told her, "and come back here." "I don't have a husband," she answered. "You have correctly said, 'I don't have a husband,'" Jesus said. "For you've had five husbands, and the man you now have is not your husband. What you have said is true." "Sir," the woman replied, "I see that you are a prophet. Our fathers worshiped on this mountain, but you Jews say that the place to worship is in Jerusalem." Jesus told her, "Believe me, woman, an hour is coming when you will worship the Father neither on this mountain nor in Jerusalem. You Samaritans worship what you do not know. We worship what we do know, because salvation is from the Jews. But an hour is coming, and is now here, when the true worshipers will worship the Father in Spirit and in truth. Yes, the Father wants such people to worship him. God is spirit, and those who worship him must worship in Spirit and in truth." The woman said to him, "I know that the Messiah is coming" (who is called Christ). "When he comes, he will explain everything to us." Jesus told her, "I, the one speaking to you, am he."

–John 4:1-26 (CSB)

Jesus knew that this woman was struggling. He knew that she wasn't fulfilled and wasn't content. She came to the well at the hottest hour of the day when she knew that no one else would be there for her to have to talk to, and she wouldn't have to deal with the talking and gossiping about her. She wouldn't have to feel the guilt and shame of what she had done, and wouldn't have to be reminded that she wasn't fulfilled, even though so many other people seemed like they were fulfilled in their lives. She runs into Jesus and He tells her that He knows where she can get living water from. Living water that will quench her thirst forever. Living water that will fulfill her and make her content and cause her to become a well of living water that could spring out onto others.

This is a woman that has been struggling with the thirst of unfulfillment and discontentment for a long time, and she lets Jesus know that she wants this living water that He can provide. Jesus then makes a peculiar demand of her and tells her to bring her husband with her. She tells him she doesn't have a husband, and Jesus says, "You have answered correctly." He knows she doesn't have a husband, and He lets her know that He knows she has been married five times, and is currently with a man she isn't married to.

Perhaps Jesus was testing her to see if she would respond with honesty and vulnerability; to know if she was ready for the conversation that they were about to have. He then tells her that He is the Messiah at the end of the conversation. I believe that Jesus is letting this woman know that the reason she is thirsty and isn't fulfilled or content is because her source of quenching her thirst, her source of fulfillment and contentment, has been her relationships with other men, and He wants her to know that it will never work! The only thing that will work is a relationship with the Messiah, Jesus Christ. She needs to make her source, The Source.

So, how can we practically do this in our marriages? Here are seven practical things we can do to make sure that we are trusting *The Source* to be our source in our marriage:

- **Read the Bible separately and together, and talk about what the Lord is teaching you.**
- **Worship together by attending a local church.**
- **As a couple, get into a community with other couples who are believers.**
- **Serve together in the community and in the church.**

- Establish some God-honoring family traditions where things are more about others than about yourselves.
- Make sure all expectations are spoken, realistic, and agreed to.
- Pray together!!! (It has been statistically proven that couples who pray together really do stay together at a much higher rate than those who don't!)

Matthew 6:33 says this:

> But seek first the kingdom of God and his righteousness, and all these things will be provided for you.
>
> (CSB)

If we will do this and focus on our relationship with God and growing in our relationship with God, I believe that we will naturally grow closer together and will be fulfilled, content, and have our thirst quenched!

- What is the secret to contentment?
- Write out what your top 5 priorities should be and what your top 5 priorities are according to your calendar and checking account and compare them. Where do you need a change?
- Do you struggle with the Messiah Complex or the Reverse Messiah Complex?
- Do you struggle with source confusion? What steps do you need to take today?

Chapter 6

Selflessness

Imagine for a second that you are sitting on the couch one Saturday afternoon watching your favorite football team. They are playing their rival, and if they win this game and then win their conference championship game, they will make the College Football Playoff, and have a chance to win the national championship. The game has just started the third quarter and was tied at halftime. Your wife sits down beside you and says that she really wants to spend some time with you because you haven't had a lot of time together lately. She wants you to go to a local coffee shop (with no TVs) and hang out together and take a board game to play. What is your first thought?

My first thought would be to make sure she knew how important this game was and that I only get to watch my favorite football team play 13-14 times a year, that we are having a good season and could go to the national championship, and I don't want to miss the game, but I would love for us to "spend some quality time together" watching the game.

Why is that my first thought? Because I'm selfish! And so are you! One of the things that made Jesus so counter-cultural and so different was the fact that he was the opposite of selfish. He was selfless. I think this is one of the most important traits for us to dig into in order for our marriages to reach their potential.

Jesus exhibited selflessness from the very beginning of his earthly life by leaving the perfection of heaven and all of his rights behind, and coming down to an imperfect earth as a vulnerable baby. He came with no pomp and circumstance and wasn't born in a palace, but was born in an old, humble, tumbledown stable with no one around but his parents and the animals.

The Apostle Paul lets us in on the selfless attitude of Jesus in the book that he wrote to the Church in Philippi, and I think we would serve ourselves and our spouses well if we did everything we could to follow Jesus' example:

> *If then there is any encouragement in Christ, if any consolation of love, if any fellowship with the Spirit, if any affection and mercy, make my joy complete by thinking the same way, having the same love, united in spirit, intent on one purpose. Do nothing out of selfish ambition or conceit, but in humility consider others as more important than yourselves. Everyone should look out not only for his own interests, but also for the interests of others. Adopt the same attitude as that of Christ Jesus, who, existing in the form of God, did not consider equality with God as something to be exploited. Instead he emptied himself by assuming the form of a servant, taking on the likeness of humanity. And when he had come as a man, he humbled himself by becoming obedient to the point of death—even to death on a cross. For this reason God highly exalted him and gave him the name that is above every name, so that at the name of Jesus every knee will bow—in heaven and on earth and under the earth—and every tongue will confess that Jesus Christ is Lord, to the glory of God the Father.*
>
> –Philippians 2:1-11 (CSB)

This Scripture tells us that we are to do nothing out of selfish ambition or conceit. This means we are to do nothing that is only about caring for ourselves, getting our way, putting our interests, benefits, and welfare above others. Instead, we are to live in humility. I have heard several people say, "Humility isn't thinking less of yourself, but it is thinking of yourself less." It isn't having a low self-confidence, but it is just thinking about others and putting others before yourself constantly. We are told by Paul to consider others as more important than ourselves and look out not only for our own interests, but also for the interests of others. Think about how this would change our marriages if we simply lived by these words more often.

Paul then goes on to tell us to have the same attitude that Jesus had. The things that characterized the attitude of Jesus were a willingness to give up everything He had for the betterment of others. He could have very easily stayed in heaven, and exploited His equality with God and not put others before Himself. However, He emptied Himself of all His privileges and rights in heaven, assuming the form of a servant when the incarnation happened, and became a man.

His humility and obedience did not end there, because as a man He was humble and obedient to the point of being willing to endure unimaginable pain, humiliation, and loneliness on the cross so that we could experience salvation, eternal life, abundant life, freedom, and victory over sin and death.

We are then told because of His humility, God then exalted Him and gave Him the name above every name and one day every knee will bow and every tongue will confess that He is Lord! God thinks that humility, sacrifice, and obedience is a huge deal, and I believe that if we live this kind of life, then God will take care of lifting us up and exalting us in His time! I think there are two huge ways we can accomplish this inside our marriages. We can love what our spouses love, and we can show our spouses love in the way that they best receive love.

The first one is pretty simple in nature, but very difficult to do. One of the things that my wife loves to do is to shop. She gets it honestly, as I have never known a family to love shopping as much as her family does. It's almost to the point of addiction with some of her family members.

The crazy thing is that sometimes they will shop for an entire day, hours on hours on hours, and they will buy NOTHING! One of the things I hate more than anything in the world is SHOPPING. I used to look for every opportunity to get out of shopping when her family would go shopping, and if I did end up having to go, I was miserable the entire time. I would sit down and read wherever we went, or look at articles, scores or social media on my phone, or text people. I would do anything I could to not have to be present in that moment because I hated it.

It is very difficult for me to enjoy and be present while we are shopping, but because my wife loves it, I need to try to love it as well. Even if I don't love it, I need to be willing to do it with a smile on my face, and fully engage in the moment, not because we are shopping, but because I'm with my wife and that's what you do if you are putting the interests of someone else above your own.

Similarly, I love sports. My wife likes sports, but she doesn't LOVE sports. She will watch our teams play, but she definitely doesn't want to watch other teams play that she doesn't know anything about or could care less about. She doesn't want to spend an entire Saturday watching College Gameday beginning at 9 AM through the last ABC game which normally ends around 11:30 PM.

However, she knows that I love sports, so from time to time she will spend a whole day watching football, or an entire

Friday watching March Madness, not because she loves sports, but because she loves me, loves being with me, and wants to live a selfless life.

So, love what they love, and it will go a long way towards making selflessness happen in your marriage. The second thing is to show your spouse love in the way that they receive love. Gary Chapman wrote a book called *The Five Love Languages*, which I can't recommend to you highly enough! You can also go to his website 5lovelanguages.com in order to see what your love languages are. In his book, he said the five love languages are as follows:

- **Words of Affirmation**—this language uses words to affirm other people.
- **Acts of Service**—for these people, actions speak louder than words.
- **Receiving Gifts**—for some people, what makes them feel most loved is to receive a gift.
- **Quality Time**—this language is all about giving the other person your undivided attention.
- **Physical Touch**—to this person, nothing speaks more deeply than appropriate touch.

The thing that makes this task difficult is that many times two people that are married have very different love languages. I have seen this play out in my parent's marriage and in our marriage.

I believe that this is one of the biggest things my parents didn't do, and one of the things that I ultimately believe led to my mom's affair and to their divorce. You don't have to be around my mom very long to know that she is a quality time and physical touch person. She loves to give hugs to everyone she sees, and all you have to do to make her happy is to spend time with her. She doesn't care about gifts, doesn't really care about you encouraging her, and could care less if you did things to help her or serve her.

Growing up, my dad saw his main responsibility as being the provider for our family. He was going to make sure that we had everything we needed, and most things that we wanted. This meant that he worked ALL THE TIME. I have always known my dad to work 14 hour days, 5 days a week, and on Saturdays 6-8 hour days.

He believed that the way he showed our family how much he loved us was to work hard and provide for us. As soon as he got home on Saturdays, it was out in the yard for several hours to cut grass, weed eat, leaf blow, trim bushes, put out pine straw, etc. He believed that he was showing us love by serving us and making sure that we had a yard that was always looking immaculate!

You might have guessed it by now, but my dad is an acts of service person. The way to my dad's heart is hard work and doing things for him around the house. I never felt like he was proud of me more than when I could finally cut grass on my own. At night, my mom was typically doing something at church and my dad was at the ball field, or if we were home my dad was watching what he wanted in the living room and my mom was watching what she wanted in their bedroom.

The problem that my parents never figured out, was that they were showing each other love in the way that they received love and not in the way that each other received love. My dad was doing all of these things thinking that he was showing my mom love, and my mom was thinking that she was showing my dad love by hugging him, holding his hand, and spending time with him. I really believe if my mom would have shown my dad love through acts of service, and if my dad would have shown my mom love by spending quality time with her, holding her hand, and hugging her more they wouldn't have ended up where they did.

Erin and I learned this lesson in our first year of marriage. One day, Erin went shopping (surprise, surprise) with her mom for a few hours. So, I decided that I was going to work like crazy in the yard (I hate yard work) so that when Erin came back, our yard would be immaculate and she would be so impressed and feel so loved that she would immediately throw me on the bed and take advantage of me when she got home. I went out in the yard and I cut grass, weed eated, blew off the driveway, planted some flowers in our flower bed, put out pine straw and trimmed the bushes. I got done several hours later, and went inside to take a shower and get a cold drink of water. I hadn't been out of the shower for very long when Erin came home. I was sitting in the living room, and she walked in and put her shopping bags on the bed. She showed me all the stuff that she bought and then we sat down in the living room together.

She said NOTHING about the yard.

Thirty minutes went by, and still nothing. Finally, after about an hour with nothing said, I asked her "Did you notice anything when you pulled in?" She responded with, "No, I don't think so." I told her she should go to the window and look outside and tell me what she saw, so she did.

She came back and said, "Oh yeah, you cut the grass. Thank you." I responded by letting her know that I didn't just cut the grass. I also weed eated, blew off the driveway, planted flowers, put out pine straw, and trimmed the bushes. I knew then that yard work, or really any household chore was the way to my heart, but not the way to Erin's heart.

Erin is a quality time and physical touch type of person. She loves to spend time doing anything together as long as we can talk and have conversation. I learned that quality time is not sitting on the couch watching TV beside each other.

There has to be some meaningful engagement. She also loves when I hold her hand, or give her an unexpected hug. Those mean way more to her than me unloading and re-loading the dishwasher 100 times.

I am an acts of service and words of affirmation type of person. I love it when I come home to a clean house, and I love it when Erin tells me how awesome I am. I could care less if she holds my hand in public or not, or brings me some type of gift. It is natural for all of us to show love in the way we receive love, but in order to be selfless and show your spouse you love them, you must do the unnatural. You must show them love in the way that they receive love. If your love languages are different, then this will be hard and difficult to do, but well worth it. Jesus being humble, coming to earth and putting our needs above His own wasn't easy, but it was worth it.

Let's fight our selfish tendencies by loving what our spouse loves, and showing them love in the way they receive love. Let's fight to have the same attitude as Christ Jesus, to not be selfish, but to be selfless, and watch how God lifts up, exalts, and takes care of our marriage!

- **When do you struggle the most with being selfless in marriage?**
- **What can you do this week with your spouse that they love?**
- **Go to 5lovelanguages.com. What is your love language and what is your spouse's love language? How can you show them love in that way this week?**

Chapter 7

Love

Love. It's something we all want. It's something we all desire. It's something that we dream about so many times growing up. We all want to fall in love, have butterflies in our stomach, and have a strong passion, desire, and emotion towards that one person for the rest of our lives.

Then, it happens. We find the person that God puts in our path. We fall in love with them. When we see them, butterflies fill our stomach. We talk on the phone for hours on end. We have such a strong passion and emotion for them. We think this is going to last for the rest of our lives. We date, get engaged, get married and then a few years later the divorce comes.

What happened? "I fell out of love with them." "I didn't love them anymore." "I still love them, I'm just not *in love* with them." The word 'love' has gotten misconstrued in our society to a point where we love everything. We love pizza. We love TV. We love sports. We love our job. We love a restaurant. We love the movies. We love country music. We love this singer, or this actor.

We love so many things, because we only have one word for love in English, and we use it so flippantly for everything. More than that, in our society the word love is used for our feeling or emotion towards something. All the examples that were just listed, the word love is used to describe a positive feeling or emotion towards each thing. I don't think that's what God had in mind when He talked about the love between a man and a wife.

When God talked about the love between a man and a wife, He used the word agape. He used the same word that described the love between God and His kids. It's a love that doesn't go away. It's a love that can't be broken. It's a love that is chosen every day. It's a love that is covenantal and not contractual. It's a love that loves even when we are faithless. It's a love that loves even when we run away. It's a love that pursues. It's a love that sacrifices. That's the kind of love that God desires between a husband and wife.

In our society we have replaced agape to describe the love between a husband and a wife with the Greek word eros. It's a love that is a feeling, that is an emotion, that is based on lust, passion, and external things. That's not the type of love that is going to keep you together for the rest of your life. That is a romantic love that will happen in different seasons of your marriage, but if your marriage is truly based on this type of love, it won't make it.

True love is not a feeling. True love is not an emotion. True love is not infatuation. True love is a commitment. True love is a daily choice. True love is mature. True love is based on eternity and not on temporary things. We put our eternal relationship with God first, and therefore we love our spouse in a more mature kind of way, because loving our spouse in that way is one of the tangible ways we can show our love of God on this Earth.

Our spirits crave God, and our spouses can't be that. So, love God unconditionally, and allow Him to work through you so that you can love your spouse unconditionally with an agape type of love. You can love God by loving your spouse this way. The Bible says it like this:

> If anyone says, "I love God," and yet hates his
> brother or sister, he is a liar. For the person
> who does not love his brother or sister whom

> *he has seen cannot love God whom he has not
> seen. And we have this command from him: the
> one who loves God must also love his brother
> and sister.*
>
> –1 John 4:20-21 (CSB)

One of the ways that we love God is by loving others, and our marriage is a perfect opportunity to do this! If all this is true, then how do we practically show love to our spouse? There are a couple of Scriptures that can teach us what this kind of mature love inside of our marriages should look like.

On the night before Jesus was going to be crucified, He wanted to have one last meal with His 12 disciples. During this last meal, we see Jesus do something that was un-ordinary for someone of His societal standing to do, as it was normally left for slaves and servants. We see Him washing the disciples' feet. The disciples thought that it was beneath them to wash other people's feet. They were too important for that. There were other people who were supposed to do that for them. If this kind of feet-washing service is beneath you, then good leadership anywhere, including the home, is above you! Here is what the Bible says:

> *Before the Passover Festival, Jesus knew that
> his hour had come to depart from this world to
> the Father. Having loved his own who were in
> the world, he loved them to the end. Now when
> it was time for supper, the devil had already
> put it into the heart of Judas, Simon Iscariot's
> son, to betray him. Jesus knew that the Father
> had given everything into his hands, that he
> had come from God, and that he was going
> back to God. So he got up from supper, laid*

aside his outer clothing, took a towel, and tied it around himself. Next, he poured water into a basin and began to wash his disciples' feet and to dry them with the towel tied around him. He came to Simon Peter, who asked him, "Lord, are you going to wash my feet?" Jesus answered him, "What I'm doing you don't realize now, but afterward you will understand." "You will never wash my feet," Peter said. Jesus replied, "If I don't wash you, you have no part with me." Simon Peter said to him, "Lord, not only my feet, but also my hands and my head." "One who has bathed," Jesus told him, "doesn't need to wash anything except his feet, but he is completely clean. You are clean, but not all of you." For he knew who would betray him. This is why he said, "Not all of you are clean." When Jesus had washed their feet and put on his outer clothing, he reclined again and said to them, "Do you know what I have done for you? You call me Teacher and Lord—and you are speaking rightly, since that is what I am. So if I, your Lord and Teacher, have washed your feet, you also ought to wash one another's feet. For I have given you an example, that you also should do just as I have done for you.

—John 13:1-15 (CSB)

It says that Jesus loved his disciples to the very end, and in order to show that, He washed their feet. He then tells us at the end of the passage that He has done this to give us an example of how we should love! I think there are four things that we can learn about real, mature love from this story.

- **Real love is hard work.** Washing the disciples feet was hard work. Jesus was already reclining at the table, so He had to get up from His reclined position, take off His outer clothing, lay it aside, take a towel and wrap it around His waist, take the water basin, pour the water in it, and then go around the room washing everyone's feet. Love is hard work! It is hard work to get up everyday and make the choice to love your spouse over any other human relationship. It is hard to make the choice to stay committed when times get hard. It is hard to say, "No matter what, I'm not leaving."

- **Real love is messy.** It wasn't a clean task for Jesus to wash the disciples' feet. Many times people in His culture walked around barefoot, and when they didn't, they had sandals on. Every time I am in flip flops on the beach, the sand gets everywhere, all over my feet and my shoes. The same thing would have been true at this time. They were walking on dirt roads that would have been filled with animal waste and maybe even human waste. I'm sure there were people who peed on the side of the road like I grew up doing in the country. Washing their feet would have been messy and disgusting. True love is messy sometimes as well. In order to choose love every day, you have to get down in the mess and work through things. You have to be able to forgive, communicate, and do the hard work of reconciliation. It can be messy, but it's worth it!

- **Real love is not deserved.** The disciples of Jesus did nothing to deserve the Savior of the World washing their feet. Our spouse doesn't necessarily do anything to deserve love. We love them because God asks us to. We love them because we are loving God by loving them. It doesn't matter if they love us back, how they treat us, or if we deem them worthy or deserving. Our job is to make the choice to love everyday regardless of what they do. Remember, you can only control what you can control. So choose to love everyday, and everything else will take care of itself.

- **Real love is not paid back.** Jesus' disciples would never be able to repay Him for the way that He loved them. He loved them by washing their feet, and they would not be returning the favor to Him. He also loved them by dying for them, and they could never repay that either. Showing love isn't about doing something so something is done in return for us. It's not about doing something hoping that we will get payment for it later. It's loving by making a choice, even if they can't or won't pay you back. Jesus tells us in other verses that even people who don't believe in Christ love people who love them back, or do good for people who can pay them back. One of the things that sets believers apart is that we are supposed to love and go the extra mile for people who can't pay us back, and even those who are considered our enemies. Real love has nothing to do with reciprocation. Real love is not giving in order to get something back. It's doing it just because you love them, and because it's what people who love one another do.

Real love is hard work. Real love is messy. Real love isn't deserved. Real love isn't paid back. Now that we have an understanding of what real love will take, why don't we look at what true love looks like.

1 Corinthians 13 is used in so many weddings, even though the text has nothing to do with a wedding. It does, however, in the middle of talking about spiritual gifts, tell us that without love, it doesn't matter how gifted we are, and then it describes what love is. I think we can take this list and use it to define true love. Here is what Paul says to the church at Corinth:

Love is patient, love is kind. Love does not envy, is not boastful, is not arrogant, is not rude, is not self-seeking, is not irritable, and does not keep a record of wrongs. Love finds no joy in unrighteousness but rejoices in the truth. It bears all things, believes all things, hopes all things, endures all things. Love never ends. But as for prophecies, they will come to an end; as for tongues, they will cease; as for knowledge, it will come to an end. For we know in part, and we prophesy in part, but when the perfect comes, the partial will come to an end. When I was a child, I spoke like a child, I thought like a child, I reasoned like a child. When I became a man, I put aside childish things. For now we see only a reflection as in a mirror, but then face to face. Now I know in part, but then I will know fully, as I am fully known. Now these three remain: faith, hope, and love—but the greatest of these is love.

–1 Corinthians 13:4-13 (CSB)

Real love is making the choice to do these things on a daily basis. It's making the decision to be patient, kind, to not be envious, to not boast or be arrogant, to not be rude, to not be all about yourself, to not be irritable, to not keep a record of the wrong things done to you, to rejoice in truth and not in unrighteousness, to withstand all things, believe in all things, hope in all things, and endure in all things, and to realize that real love will never end! Those are not some easy choices to make, but they are well worth it!

If you are currently dissatisfied in your marriage because you don't love your spouse anymore, repent, or begin to think differently about love, and realize it's not a feeling or emotion, but a choice. It's a choice that you can make today and every day for the rest of your life!

- **How can you show true love to your spouse this week?**
- **What are the characteristics of true love?**

Chapter 8

Sex

This is the part of the book that everyone comes to a marriage book looking for. A chapter on sex. Sex is a big part of marriage, it's just not the most important part like everyone thinks it is. Sex is also way more difficult, and happens less than you grew up thinking, because of TV shows or movies, or because of what you heard from others. We are going to talk about it because God's Word talks about it.

Sex has been a part of marriage since the very beginning. God told Adam and Eve to be fruitful and multiply. The only way that can happen is by having sex. Sex is a gift, and if done in the correct boundaries, it is a way that we can worship God. God has given us these desires because sex is an important part of obeying God's command to become one flesh with the person you marry.

The process of becoming one flesh is not just based on physical intimacy, but it is a huge part of becoming one, along with emotional and spiritual intimacy. The couple who is spiritually intimate, emotionally intimate, and physically intimate will have an incredible foundation for a thriving marriage!

Sex can be a wonderful, fulfilling, exciting gift as long as it is kept in the right boundaries. Outside of that it can be disastrous and destructive. God wants sex inside of marriage to be fun, passionate, and intimate, but our enemy wants us to believe differently. Our enemy wants us to believe that sex inside of marriage is boring, monotonous, and almost nonexistent, but sex outside of marriage is fun, exciting, and normal.

Sex is a lot like fire. When a fire is confined to the proper boundaries such as a fireplace or fire pit, it is powerful, beautiful, and full of warmth. However, if it gets outside of those boundaries it can be disastrous, destructive, and can ruin houses, ruin land, and kill people.

We look at boundaries as bad things because we think it takes away from our freedoms. However, boundaries are good things for us because God knows exactly how we were created to work for our joy, the world's good, and His glory, and that's why boundaries exist: to help us to know and learn how we were created to operate.

We see warnings all throughout Scripture. The Bible is full of passages that tell us to flee sexual immorality. When Joseph, who was second in command in Egypt, goes into Potiphar's house and finds Potiphar's wife standing there without much on and no one else in the house, and she is begging him to sleep with her, he could have easily done that. Maybe no one would have found out.

However, Joseph decided that he would rather trade short-term pleasure and worldly success for long-term faithfulness and obedience to God, so he ran out of the house and fled. She lied about what happened and he got thrown in jail, but God was always with him, always used him for good even in difficult times, and eventually Joseph received everything that he had and more because of his faithfulness to God.

Jesus, in his famous Sermon on the Mount in Matthew 5, tells us that if our eyes and/or hands cause us to sin in a sexual way, we will be better to gouge our eye out or cut our hand off than to entertain sexual immorality. James tells us that we are tempted by our evil desires, and when we take action on those desires it turns to sin, and when sin is full grown, it gives birth to death. We must realize that outside of its intended boundaries, sex can be very disastrous and destructive. We must heed the Bible's warnings and trust that God knows what He is talking about.

I believe that we take sex and the potential disaster and destruction it can bring way too lightly. We compartmentalize it and say things like, "I'm just window shopping. I'm not actually going to do anything about it. I can manage it. I can quit anytime I want to. It's no big deal. No one will ever find out." The enemy uses these thoughts to get us to take action on these desires, and then they become sin, and if entertained for too long, sin can become death. Death spiritually, death to relationships, death to careers, death of peace and joy, and possibly death physically.

We have to make the decision to completely do away with it. I read a book recently titled, "What Radical Husbands Do", by Regi Campbell. He tells the story about a Spanish conquistador who forced his men to burn the ships when they reached the island they were sailing for, because he knew their chances of success were much higher if retreating wasn't even an option.

This is how we must treat sex. We must burn and get rid of anything sexual outside of marriage, because it's much easier to stay faithful and obedient if there aren't other options. If you struggle with pornography, get a flip phone and get rid of your computer at home, or get software that will keep you accountable on all of your devices. If you struggle with calling sex lines, let someone else see your call log every month. If you struggle with people of the opposite sex, then put people around yourself to help hold you accountable, and make sure to put up healthy boundaries so you aren't even tempted. What ships do you need to burn so that things don't become disastrous?

The other thing that will help us stay pure comes right from God's Word. Psalm 119:9 says:

How can a young man keep his way pure? By keeping your word.

(CSB)

Reading the Bible helps us stay pure. It's much easier to be obedient and faithful to God if I am listening to Him speak to me through His Word every single day. Read God's Word. Study God's Word. Meditate on God's Word. Memorize God's Word. These things will help you stay pure.

When Jesus was faced with temptation from the enemy, He used God's Word to fend the enemy off and send him away without falling for any of his schemes. The Word of God is called a double edged sword, and is the only offensive weapon against the enemy that we are given. So why wouldn't we use it?! Let's get in God's Word daily, and trust that God in His power will help us stay pure!

Let's take a look together at a few passages of Scripture that talk directly about sex inside of marriage so we can know what the Bible has to say about having a healthy sex life! Paul says the following to the church at Corinth, but when you read it you realize that some of the same struggles happening in Corinth are also happening in America today, so I think it is a good passage for us to look at:

But because sexual immorality is so common, each man should have sexual relations with his own wife, and each woman should have sexual relations with her own husband. A husband should fulfill his marital duty to his wife, and likewise a wife to her husband. A wife does not have the right over her own body, but her husband does. In the same way, a husband does not have the right over his own body, but his wife does. Do not deprive one another—except when you agree for a time, to devote yourselves to prayer. Then come together again; otherwise, Satan may tempt you because of your lack of self-control.

–1 Corinthians 7:2-5 (CSB)

It is part of our marital duty to please each other sexually. This means that both husbands and wives should initiate it, and say yes many times, even if we don't feel like it. We aren't supposed to use sex against each other, or deprive each other unless it is agreed upon for a short period of time to devote ourselves to prayer. It says that by doing this we won't give Satan a chance to tempt us!

If we are going to look at what Scripture has to say on the context of sex, we must look at a couple of passages from the Song of Solomon, which in my opinion, is the best book on sex ever written. Here is what is said in Chapter 4:

Man: *How beautiful you are, my darling. How very beautiful! Behind your veil, your eyes are doves. Your hair is like a flock of goats streaming down Mount Gilead. Your teeth are like a flock of newly shorn sheep coming up from washing, each one bearing twins, and none has lost its young. Your lips are like a scarlet cord, and your mouth is lovely. Behind your veil, your brow is like a slice of pomegranate. Your neck is like the tower of David, constructed in layers. A thousand shields are hung on it—all of them shields of warriors. Your breasts are like two fawns, twins of a gazelle, that feed among the lilies. Until the day breaks and the shadows flee,*

I will make my way to the mountain of myrrh and the hill of frankincense. You are absolutely beautiful, my darling; there is no imperfection in you. Come with me from Lebanon, my bride; come with me from Lebanon! Descend from the peak of Amana, from the summit of Senir and Hermon, from the dens of the lions, from the mountains of the leopards. You have captured my heart, my sister, my bride. You have captured my heart with one glance of your eyes, with one jewel of your necklace. How delightful your caresses are, my sister, my bride. Your caresses are much better than wine, and the fragrance of your perfume than any balsam. Your lips drip sweetness like the honeycomb, my bride. Honey and milk are under your tongue. The fragrance of your garments is like the fragrance of Lebanon. My sister, my bride, you are a locked garden—a locked garden and a sealed spring. Your branches are a paradise of pomegranates with choicest fruits; henna with nard, nard and saffron, calamus and cinnamon, with all the trees of frankincense, myrrh and aloes, with all the best spices. You are a garden spring, a well of flowing water streaming from Lebanon.

Woman: *Awaken, north wind; come, south wind. Blow on my garden, and spread the fragrance of its spices. Let my love come to his garden and eat its choicest fruits.*

–Song of Solomon 4:1-16 (CSB)

I think we can learn several things from this passage of Scripture. The first three chapters of this book, he spends building the foundation of their relationship before he ever gets to the sexual part. We must realize that a good foundation in our marriage is vital, and we must focus on our soul and our spouse before we ever begin to focus on sex. When he does get to Chapter 4 and he begins talking about sex, he does so in a very gentle way. It doesn't appear that he is in a rush like most men are. He takes his time, goes from the top of her body to the bottom, takes in her beauty and dignity, and celebrates it—he spends some time flirting with her first.

You have heard the saying that men are like microwaves and women are like crockpots. There is a lot of truth to that statement, as it sometimes takes a bit of time to get a woman warmed up. Husbands must be the best flirters around, not with other women, but with their wives. Take some time to build anticipation. Send her flirty texts and little comments and include some bitmojis, emojis, and gifs throughout the day so that when nighttime hits, she is just as excited as you are!

Not only is he taking his time and not rushing, he is also speaking life into her. He is showing that he cares for her, is putting her first, and is focused on giving to her and caring for her more than he is focused on getting something for himself. He makes it about her person and her soul, not just about physical sex.

Our relationships can't be built on just the physical. Physical attraction is good and a gift, but it's dangerous if it's the foundation. Sex and pleasure will never fully nourish your soul, because every fleshly hunger is actually something that can spiritually be met by God even better.

There are so many seasons to marriage, such as pregnancy, sickness, kids, etc., but if your relationship is not built on sex then you can still have intimacy during these times. Make sure you are pursuing your spouse, speaking life to them, and valuing their soul over their body, and the spiritual over the physical. The best sex always starts with honesty in the living room. Honesty and connection lead to intimacy in the most important things, and that will lead to physical intimacy! That is the fuel that will keep the fire going.

The man in this chapter refuses to take her until she offers herself up to him, and he spends 16 verses speaking life into her before she offers herself up to him. However, when she offers, she is all in because he has done all of the most important things first.

I heard a pastor give this advice once, and I think it's something good and practical to try. Husbands, burn a CD, or create a playlist with 10 songs on it. The first three songs don't go below the chin. The next three songs don't go below the waist. Song 7 is the "go" song. The last three songs are for cuddling. I hope this helps! The last passage we will look at in Song of Solomon comes from chapter 7:

> **Man:** *How beautiful are your sandaled feet, princess! The curves of your thighs are like jewelry, the handiwork of a master. Your navel is a rounded bowl; it never lacks mixed wine. Your belly is a mound of wheat surrounded by lilies. Your breasts are like two fawns, twins of a gazelle. Your neck is like a tower of ivory, your eyes like pools in Heshbon by Bath-rabbim's gate. Your nose is like the tower of Lebanon looking toward Damascus. Your head crowns you like Mount Carmel, the hair of your head like purple cloth—a king could be held captive in your tresses. How beautiful you are and how*

pleasant, my love, with such delights! Your stature is like a palm tree; your breasts are clusters of fruit. I said, "I will climb the palm tree and take hold of its fruit." May your breasts be like clusters of grapes, and the fragrance of your breath like apricots. Your mouth is like fine wine—

Woman: *flowing smoothly for my love, gliding past my lips and teeth! I am my love's, and his desire is for me. Come, my love, let's go to the field; let's spend the night among the henna blossoms. Let's go early to the vineyards; let's see if the vine has budded, if the blossom has opened, if the pomegranates are in bloom. There I will give you my caresses. The mandrakes give off a fragrance, and at our doors is every delicacy, both new and old. I have treasured them up for you, my love.*

–Song of Solomon 7:1-13 (CSB)

This time, he begins with her feet. I wouldn't recommend using some of these same compliments for your spouse today, but maybe in that day and time these were flattering. I wouldn't tell your spouse that their belly button is a rounded bowl and that their belly is a mound of wheat. I also wouldn't tell them that their nose is like a tower. We can definitely tell from the two chapters we have read in Song of Solomon that he had a appreciation for necks and breasts.

There are definitely some things that we can take from this love story. I love that this chapter has them spending time together and enjoying each other. One of the benefits to being married and having sex is that you spend a lot of time together and you get to see and learn things about your spouse that no one else sees and knows. We can encourage those things in our spouse, and we can use those things to serve our spouse.

If both husband and wife focus on serving each other based on things they learn about each other inside and outside the bedroom, they will have great sex. Married sex means that we can just learn each other and make sex more frequent and enjoyable. The more it happens, the more we will enjoy it and want it to happen.

We must fight to be students of each other, to pay attention to each other, and to build a friendship where we desire to spend time with each other! Fight for fun and fight for romance. Proverbs 5 says:

> *Let your fountain be blessed, and take pleasure in the wife of your youth. A loving deer, a graceful doe—let her breasts always satisfy you; be lost in her love forever.*
> *–Proverbs 5:18-19 (CSB)*

There should be joy, pleasure, and enjoyment in our marriages.

Lastly, I will say that communication is key in marriage, and it's key in our sex lives. We have to be able to talk to our spouse about our sex life. Talk about your likes and dislikes, talk about your expectations, and talk about it constantly.

There is a huge problem if you talk more to your girlfriends or poker buddies than you do to your spouse about your sex life. This is an intimate and private part of your marriage. Getting advice from a counselor or trusted friend is one thing, but openly discussing details and likes and dislikes with others doesn't build trust between you and your spouse. Great intimacy comes from great communication, so let's talk about it!

- What do you need to get rid of in your life?
- How can you increase the intimacy between you and your spouse spiritually, mentally, emotionally, and physically?
- What can you do to make reading the Bible a normal habit in your life?
- What do you need to tell your spouse about your expectations, wants, and needs sexually? Tell them!

Chapter 9

Communication

Have you ever had a miscommunication with your spouse? Have you ever said one thing, but they took it differently than you meant it? Have you ever expected something, communicated it, and it didn't happen? Have you ever assumed something would take place, and it didn't? Have you ever gotten angry because your spouse didn't meet an expectation that you never spoke?

It all boils down to communication. I believe that communication is the key in marriage. I believe that it's the oxygen that helps marriages stay alive. We are going to look at a couple passages of Scripture, and then some practical ways we can communicate successfully with our spouse. The first thing that we must do is realize how much power there is in our words and our communication. James says this:

> *Not many should become teachers, my brothers, because you know that we will receive a stricter judgment. For we all stumble in many ways. If anyone does not stumble in what he says, he is mature, able also to control the whole body. Now if we put bits into the mouths of horses so that they obey us, we direct their whole bodies. And consider ships: though very large and driven by fierce winds, they are guided by a very small rudder wherever the will of the pilot directs. So too, though the tongue is a small part of the body, it boasts great things.*

Consider how a small fire sets ablaze a large forest. And the tongue is a fire. The tongue, a world of unrighteousness, is placed among our members. It stains the whole body, sets the course of life on fire, and is itself set on fire by hell. Every kind of animal, bird, reptile, and fish is tamed and has been tamed by humankind, but no one can tame the tongue. It is a restless evil, full of deadly poison. With the tongue we bless our Lord and Father, and with it we curse people who are made in God's likeness. Blessing and cursing come out of the same mouth. My brothers and sisters, these things should not be this way. Does a spring pour out sweet and bitter water from the same opening? Can a fig tree produce olives, my brothers and sisters, or a grapevine produce figs? Neither can a saltwater spring yield fresh water.

–James 3:1-12 (CSB)

James says that just like horses are controlled by small bits in their mouths, ships are controlled by small rudders, and forests can be set on fire by a small spark, so it is with our tongues. They are very small, but they have so much power. We are sinful human beings and our enemy loves to use our tongues for evil, to cause fires, and to be poisonous in order to harm others. We bless God with our tongues one minute and curse others with it the next, and James tells us that this shouldn't be so. He tells us that it's impossible for a spring to pour out sweet water and bitter water from the same opening, and it's impossible for a fig tree to produce olives or a grapevine to produce figs, and it's impossible for a saltwater spring to yield fresh water.

Just like that, he says it should be impossible for our tongues to build up and praise God and also tear others down. There is a lot of power in the tongue. Proverbs 12:18 says:

> *There is one who speaks rashly, like a piercing sword; but the tongue of the wise brings healing.*
> (CSB)

Proverbs 18:21 says:

> *Death and life are in the power of the tongue, and those who love it will eat its fruit.*
> (CSB)

Once we realize how powerful the tongue and our words are, we can look for some practical advice on communication. The Apostle Paul gives us some good criteria for communication in his letter to the church at Ephesus. Here is what he says in Chapter 4:

> *Therefore, putting away lying, **speak the truth, each one to his neighbor,** because we are members of one another [emphasis added]. **Be angry and do not sin** [emphasis added]. Don't let the sun go down on your anger, and don't give the devil an opportunity. Let the thief no longer steal. Instead, he is to do honest work with his own hands, so that he has something to share with anyone in need. No foul language should come from your mouth, but only what is good for building up someone in need, so that it gives grace to those who hear. And don't grieve God's Holy Spirit. You were sealed by him for*

> *the day of redemption. Let all bitterness, anger and wrath, shouting and slander be removed from you, along with all malice. And be kind and compassionate to one another, forgiving one another, just as God also forgave you in Christ."*
>
> –Ephesians 4:25-32 (CSB)

This passage gives us several things to make sure we do in order to communicate well. We must speak the truth. The first part of great communication is honesty. We also must make sure that as we communicate, we are not sinning in our anger. Not all anger is sin unless it is your default every time you communicate with your spouse. Paul tells us not to let the sun go down on our anger so we don't give any opportunity to the devil.

We must deal with our anger, and resolve our issues before bed. The moment you don't, you go to bed mad, you wake up more mad, resentful and bitter, and it gives Satan a crack in the door to wreak havoc in your marriage. He tells us to only let talk that builds up at the right time, and gives grace to those who hear it come out of our mouth.

Our communication with our spouse should be communication that builds them up and gives them grace, not words that tear them down. He then tells us to let bitterness, wrath, anger, clamor, slander, and malice be removed from us and that we are to be kind, tenderhearted, and forgiving towards one another like Christ is to us. I think if we do these things we will communicate effectively with each other.

Now, let's talk through some practical things that you can do in order to communicate with your spouse well:

- **Prioritize leaving and coming home.** Make sure that you are intentional about your hellos and goodbyes. Look them in the eye, give them a hug and kiss, and say "I love you" when you leave and when you come home. Make sure you check your mood before entering the house, and if you need to take 5 minutes to drive around to make sure you're in a good mood, then do it!

- **Take Time.** You can't communicate effectively if you don't take time to actually communicate. This is why a date night with questions is such an important thing. If you can't get away, have some at-home date nights. Embrace healthy routines such as eating meals together as a family, around a table and not in front of a TV. (I have included some date night ideas as well as date night questions you can discuss at the end of this book.)

- **Get on the same page.** You must take time to make sure that as a couple you are on the same page and have the same expectations. One of the best things that Erin and I do is to make sure we talk about the budget every month, and every week we sit down and walk through our weekly calendars together so that there are no surprises. Go to bed together every night, and make sure you do not go to bed angry, and it will also help you stay on the same page!

- **Listen effectively.** 65% of all communication is listening. Listen with the intent of understanding, not with the intent of trying to solve their problems. Many times our spouse just wants someone to listen, not someone to solve their issues for them. Hear your spouse's point of view, and take time to really understand their heart more than seeking to be understood. You can't be right all the time *and* have a great marriage. Look them in the eyes, put the phone down, be fully engaged, and be face-to-face with them.

- **Encourage each other.** We must be willing to encourage and build our spouse up. Make sure to always give grace, to never assume the worst and to always speak the truth in love. We must not assume meaning, use sarcasm, call them names, criticize them personally, nor use the words never or always, blame them, get defensive or bring up divorce. You can tear down or build up. It's your choice.

- **Be honest.** We must be honest about how we feel. We can't shut down and stonewall and not respond. We also can't run away and escape it. Be honest with how you feel, and trust that your spouse will be understanding.
- **Understand that men and women are different.** Women tend to express and verbalize things while men like to fix things. Be a student of your spouse, study them, learn things about them, and seek to understand them more.
- **Make sure to focus on the plank in your eye, before focusing on the speck in your spouse's eye.** We all have things that we can work on, and the more time we spend focusing on ourselves, and how we can get better—asking the Lord to help us be the best spouse we can be—the better it will go for us. Instead of criticizing everything about your spouse, ask God to fix you! This also includes the fact that both people in a marriage must be willing to compromise. There are times where the best thing you can do is to not get your way, but to take both of the ideas and opinions and find a solution that is somewhere in the middle.
- **Think before you speak.** Hearing your spouse's heart is way more important than making your point or winning the argument. Ask yourself, "Should what I'm thinking be said, and should it be said right now?"
- **Read the Bible.** The Bible tells us that it is out of the overflow of the heart that the mouth speaks. Most of our communication is about our hearts, and pure hearts come from spending time with God and reading His Word.
- **Pray.** Pray with your spouse and separately. Ask God to guide your words and your heart before hard conversations.

Pray about difficult decisions. Ask the Lord to align your hearts and minds if you disagree about something. Pray during the argument (silently, of course) even when the other person seems hard to pray for. Pray for them in the morning and at night. It will help your words and thoughts to become more like Jesus!

Do these things, and I believe that you and your spouse will win in the communication department, and therefore will win in marriage! Part of great communication is great conflict, and that's what we're going to discuss next.

- **How can you use your words to build up the people around you this week?**
- **What practice can you adopt to communicate better to the people around you?**

Chapter 10

Conflict

I remember when Erin and I were dating and engaged we would get asked, "How is your relationship?" There were many times where we would answer that question with the statement, "Things are really great, we have a good time, we talk to each other a lot, and we never argue."

After being married for several years now, I realize that isn't necessarily a good thing. When I do premarital counseling for couples and they tell me during the conflict section of counseling that they don't argue or fight very much, I challenge them pretty hard, and then do everything I can to create an argument.

I have learned that if you aren't having conflict, then one person isn't saying how they truly feel and being honest. I have learned if you aren't having conflict that you might not be figuring out the best solution to certain issues. I have learned that if we have conflict in a healthy way, it can make us more like Jesus, it can help us learn more about the other person, and it can move our marriages forward. If true intimacy exists in a marriage, you will fight. When we realize that we are all sinful and selfish, we all have baggage, and that we are very different from our spouse, and because of these things we will have conflict, we will set ourselves up for success in conflict.

The first thing we must learn to conflict well is that our spouse isn't our enemy. I heard someone say, "You will fight with someone the rest of your life, who do you want it to be? Marry them!" We have an enemy, but it isn't our spouse. John 10:10 says:

> *A thief comes only to steal and kill and destroy.*
> *I have come so that they may have life and have*
> *it in abundance.*
>
> (CSB)

Our enemy wants to steal and kill and destroy our marriages, and he can do that if we do not learn to have healthy conflict. Our enemy is not our spouse, or any human being. Ephesians 6 says it this way:

> *For our struggle is not against flesh and blood,*
> *but against the rulers, against the authorities,*
> *against the cosmic powers of this darkness,*
> *against evil, spiritual forces in the heavens.*
> –Ephesians 6:12 (CSB)

Everyone fights, and you can learn to fight fair. It starts with the realization that your spouse isn't your enemy, Satan is. He doesn't want you to fight fair, because he wants to use conflict to create a wedge between you and your spouse. So, let's learn how to fight in a healthy way. I think the most important thing is to heed the words of James when he tells us:

> *My dear brothers and sisters, understand this:*
> *everyone should be quick to listen, slow to*
> *speak, and slow to anger, for human anger does*
> *not accomplish God's righteousness.*
> –James 1:19-20 (CSB)

I believe if we would listen to this seemingly simple advice, our marriages would be completely different, because our communication and conflict would be completely different. This is the way we should operate with our spouse in our marriages. We should be quick to listen and slow to speak. This is something that I personally struggle with. I am not very quick to listen or slow to speak.

If this verse was being written about me, it would say, "Quick to give my opinion, slow to hear my wife's opinion. Quick to want my point to be heard, slow to hear my wife's point. Quick to offer a solution, slow to just be a sounding board." However, if we want our communication and conflict to be healthy we must be quick to listen. Communication and healthy conflict is much more about being a good listener than anything else.

It then tells us to be slow to anger. Surprise, surprise, I'm not very good at this one either. I come from a family where anger was the norm. My dad always had a quick temper, and I was raised to think that anger was ok. It was natural, and it was how people in my family were. I have since learned that anger is a choice, but it isn't something that I have mastered yet.

Anger isn't wrong in and of itself. It is the things that anger often leads to that can be sinful. It is the yelling, the tearing down, the emotional, mental, or physical abuse that anger can lead to that is sin. We simply need to calm down, breathe, and realize that most of the things we are having conflict about are not that big of a deal in the grand scheme of things.

When you are about to enter into a conflict, or you are in the middle of conflict, here are some questions that you can ask yourself to make sure that your conflict stays healthy:

- **Is this the right time?** I have learned that timing is everything in life and in conflict. I don't recommend fighting late at night when you're tired, when you are in public, or when you are hungry. When you are tired, whatever filter you have goes away, and we tend to not think before we speak. When we are in public, you are doing it in front of other people which is not healthy. When you are hungry, well, "hanger" is a real thing. In order to have healthy conflict, you must time it right. We also cannot go to bed angry, so we must figure out a time to actually conflict. You might be saying, "The only time I see my spouse is late at night, in public, or when I am hungry—what am I supposed to do?" You have time, and can find time, you just have to realize that this is more important than whatever else it is that you are prioritizing over a healthy marriage.

- **Is this a topic worth fighting about?** Not every hill is worth dying on, but you also don't want to be running away from a conversation or avoiding a certain topic because you don't want to fight. You must figure out if whatever you are discussing is worth it and if you need to embrace it, or if you just need to let it go.

- **Am I fighting to win?** Those of you that are competitive like me will have a hard time with this one. Fighting is not a sport to try to win. The goal is resolving the conflict and our marriage moving forward, not me achieving a personal victory. Healthy couples fight for resolution, unhealthy couples fight for personal victory.

- **Am I keeping short accounts?** 1 Corinthians 13 tells us that love keeps no record of wrongs. We must not get historical when we are fighting. We need to forgive, move on, and not bring things back up. When something happens and it bothers you, bring it up immediately. You shouldn't just sit on it, stuff it, and not say anything because eventually you will erupt, and that has the potential to do some serious damage. If you are a "stuffer" you are a lot like a volcano. You may be dormant for weeks, months, maybe even years. However, when you blow, you spew lava everywhere, and you could cause some serious damage.

- **Am I raising my voice?** This has been an interesting one for me. I grew up in a family where yelling was normal. In order to be heard, you had to be the loudest. My wife grew up in a family where no one ever yelled. So, when we got married and I would get loud, Erin would tell me to stop yelling. I would then yell, "I'm not yelling!" I learned that even though I didn't think I was yelling, my wife thought I was yelling, and that meant that I was yelling. Healthy conflict is just as much about how you say it as it is what you say.

- **Am I controlling my anger?** Losing your temper is a choice. You can choose to allow yourself to lose it or not. Scripture tells us over and over that quick tempered people are fools. The book of Proverbs tells us that a person without self-control is like a city with no walls. A city with no walls in the time when Proverbs was written was a city that was vulnerable and open to the enemy's attack. The same is true for us if we cannot get a handle on our anger. If we don't control it, it will control us.

We will fight. Let's fight in a healthy way that will help us become more like Jesus, bring us closer to our spouse, and make our marriages better!

- **What do you need to do in order to do a better job of fighting fair?**
- **Do you struggle with being quick to listen, slow to speak, or being slow to become angry? How can you grow in that?**
- **What part of healthy conflict do you struggle with the most?**

Chapter 11

Two F Words

There are a lot of F words that I can think of that could play a part in our marriages. However, I can't think of two better ones than forgiveness and fun. These are also two words that I believe are lacking in a lot of marriages today.

Forgiveness

Let's look at a couple of stories from the Gospels that may tell us what forgiveness is, and how we can do it well. The first story involves Jesus, and the second story is a parable that Jesus tells to teach us about forgiveness. The first story comes out of John 8:

> *At dawn he went to the temple again, and all the people were coming to him. He sat down and began to teach them. Then the scribes and the Pharisees brought a woman caught in adultery, making her stand in the center. "Teacher," they said to him, "this woman was caught in the act of committing adultery. In the law Moses commanded us to stone such women. So what do you say?" They asked this to trap him, in order that they might have evidence to accuse him. Jesus stooped down and started writing on the ground with his finger. When they persisted in questioning*

him, he stood up and said to them, "The one without sin among you should be the first to throw a stone at her." Then he stooped down again and continued writing on the ground. When they heard this, they left one by one, starting with the older men. Only he was left, with the woman in the center. When Jesus stood up, he said to her, "Woman, where are they? Has no one condemned you?" "No one, Lord," she answered. "Neither do I condemn you," said Jesus. "Go, and from now on do not sin anymore."

–John 8:2-11 (CSB)

This story is an interesting one because it shows us how Jesus deals with someone who is caught in the middle of sin. Jesus was the only one in the story who actually had the right to dispense justice, but he treated her with compassion and forgave her, instead of condemning her. I think a lot of us are like the people who are standing around holding rocks in our hand towards our spouses. We know we aren't supposed to throw the stone at them because we are sinners too, but we aren't sure we want to completely put the rock down.

However, holding onto the rock so that you can use it later is bitterness. Holding onto bitterness will lead to resentment, and resentment will kill intimacy. True forgiveness is choosing to put down our stones. Jesus didn't just offer forgiveness to her for her to continue living like she had been living. He forgave her and told her that she had the opportunity to go and not continue in the habitual sin she had been trapped in, and therefore could earn the trust of the people around her.

Since our marriages involve two people who are sinful, falls are inevitable and we can't control that. However, we can control the direction in which we fall. We can fall toward or away from God, and we can fall toward or away from our spouse. The spiritually-immature response is to pull back, become more distant, or even start over with someone else. However, to move like God is to move towards others, including sinful people. God sent His Son into a world that hated Him for the purpose of forgiving it.

One of marriage's primary purposes is to teach us how to forgive. Ruth Bell Graham has said, "A happy marriage is the union of two good forgivers." Forgiveness is about obedience and faithfulness to a God who forgave us. It is in God's nature to forgive. His character is such that He died a brutal death for the sake of the people who abused him. It's not something that comes naturally for us, and is something that must be learned by taking the harder road. Hebrews 12 says:

> *Pursue peace with everyone, and holiness—*
> *without it no one will see the Lord. Make sure*
> *that no one falls short of the grace of God and*
> *that no root of bitterness springs up, causing*
> *trouble and defiling many.*
>
> –Hebrews 12:14-15 (CSB)

Romans 12 says:

> *Do not repay anyone evil for evil. Give careful*
> *thought to do what is honorable in everyone's*
> *eyes. If possible, as far as it depends on you, live*
> *at peace with everyone. Friends, do not avenge*
> *yourselves; instead, leave room for God's wrath,*
> *because it is written, **vengeance belongs to me;***
> ***I will repay,** says the Lord [emphasis added].*
>
> –Romans 12:17-19 (CSB)

If we want to become spiritually mature and more like Jesus, we must learn how to forgive our spouse and show them grace because we realize that revenge isn't ours to give. We can let God take care of that, and as far as we are concerned, we should pursue peace. Let's learn some things about forgiveness to help us:

- **Forgiveness is what God wants.** Forgiveness is the only way to heal. It doesn't excuse their behavior, it just keeps their behavior from destroying your heart. It brings freedom and allows us to put down the chains of bondage that unforgiveness puts us in. Forgiveness is an act of self-defense because it stops us from becoming bitter and full of resentment. It prevents us from forfeiting our future by living in the past. We will never truly live until our past dies. You aren't hurting the other person by not forgiving them, you are hurting and enslaving yourself. Sin doesn't end marriages, unforgiveness does. So, if we want our marriage to thrive then we must learn to forgive. Matthew 6 says:

  > *For if you forgive others their offenses, your heavenly Father will forgive you as well. But if you don't forgive others, your Father will not forgive your offenses.*
  >
  > Matthew 6:14-15 (CSB)

  Let's be obedient to God, and forgive because it's what He wants and is what's best for us!

- **Forgiveness is a choice.** I think the best way to see this is to look at a parable that Jesus told to teach us about forgiveness. It comes from Matthew 18 and says:

  > *Then Peter approached him and asked, "Lord, how many times shall I forgive my brother or*

sister who sins against me? As many as seven times?" "I tell you, not as many as seven," Jesus replied, "but seventy times seven. "For this reason, the kingdom of heaven can be compared to a king who wanted to settle accounts with his servants. When he began to settle accounts, one who owed ten thousand talents was brought before him. Since he did not have the money to pay it back, his master commanded that he, his wife, his children, and everything he had be sold to pay the debt. "At this, the servant fell face down before him and said, 'Be patient with me, and I will pay you everything.' Then the master of that servant had compassion, released him, and forgave him the loan. "That servant went out and found one of his fellow servants who owed him a hundred denarii. He grabbed him, started choking him, and said, 'Pay what you owe!' "At this, his fellow servant fell down and began begging him, 'Be patient with me, and I will pay you back.' But he wasn't willing. Instead, he went and threw him into prison until he could pay what was owed. When the other servants saw what had taken place, they were deeply distressed and went and reported to their master everything that had happened. Then, after he had summoned him, his master said to him, 'You wicked servant! I forgave you all that debt because you begged me. Shouldn't you also have had mercy on your fellow servant, as I had mercy on you?' And because he was angry, his master handed him over to the jailers to be tortured until he

> *could pay everything that was owed. So also*
> *my heavenly Father will do to you unless every*
> *one of you forgives his brother or sister from*
> *your heart.*
>
> –Matthew 18:21-35 (CSB)

There are a few things to note from this parable Jesus told. In Judaism, which was the religion they were raised in, three times of forgiving someone would have been sufficient to show a forgiving spirit. Peter, however, believes that he is being incredibly generous by asking if he should forgive someone seven times. That's the normal amount multiplied by 2 and then adding 1. It also is the number in Scripture that signifies completion. Peter is asking, "Should I completely forgive the person who sins against me?" Jesus then lets Peter know that completely forgiving someone one time isn't good enough. He tells him he must forgive someone seventy times seven times. In other words, you must make the choice to completely forgive them, but it's a choice you must continually make every single day. True forgiveness is complete and continual. He then tells the parable. He tells us that the first servant owes the king 10,000 talents, or about 6 billion dollars in our terms. He pleads with the king for mercy and forgiveness and the king lets him off the hook. Once the king lets him off the hook, he goes and finds another servant who owes him 100 denarii which would be about 12,000 dollars in our terms. He demands the servant pay him and when the servant pleads with him in the same way that he pleaded with the king, he doesn't let him off the hook. He instead had the servant thrown into prison until he could repay him. This gets back to the king and he summons him and calls him a wicked servant, and tells him that because the king showed him mercy that he should have shown mercy to his fellow servant. Jesus tells us this parable to instruct us as His followers. We owe a massive debt to God like the first servant because of our sin. It's a debt that we could never repay, but because of His great mercy, He completely forgave our debt by sending His Son Jesus to die on the cross for us to take care of that sin. Since God has let us off the hook and forgiven us, then we should be quick to forgive others as well. If the mercy of God has truly had a saving effect on someone, then they will be comparably merciful to others. If we are transformed by the forgiveness that God shows us, then we will extend that same forgiveness to others. It's a choice, independent of the response of the other person, and it must be continuous and complete!

- **Forgiveness is a process.** It's not something that will happen quickly or immediately all the time, but it is a process that takes time.

- **Forgiveness is releasing debt.** Jesus paid for our sin and the sin of the person who we need to forgive, so we need to put it in His hands and let Him deal with it the best way possible.

- **Forgiveness isn't ignoring the problem, forgetting it, or pretending it didn't hurt.** Forgiveness and trust aren't the same thing. Trust is something that has to be earned. You can offer forgiveness quickly, but trust slowly. We need to realize that because all humans will let us down, we can never put our full trust in the flesh of a human being. However, we can learn to trust Jesus inside of someone. The more we see someone spending time with Jesus, digging into His Word, and hearing from Him the more we can trust that person. Forgiveness is acknowledging your wound, and choosing to go through the process of grieving and forgiving.

- **Forgiveness is unconditional.** Forgiveness isn't something that we can do with conditions, expecting some kind of performance on the back end from the other party. It's not about whether they can repay you or make it up to you. It's about you forgiving regardless of what they do, and trusting Jesus for His redemption!

- **Forgiveness is possible.** In Matthew 19:26, even though the context is different, I think the words of Jesus can still apply:

> *Jesus looked at them and said, "With man this is impossible, but with God all things are possible."*

> (CSB)

Fun

Craig Groeschel says, "Too many people see fun in a marriage as a luxury. It's not a luxury, it's a requirement." So many of our marriages have become business arrangements where there is no fun. It's like our houses have big signs on them that say, "no fun allowed!" We might have fun with our kids, but do we have fun with our spouse? Ecclesiastes 9:9 says:

> *Enjoy life with the wife you love all the days of your fleeting life, which has been given to you under the sun, all your fleeting days. For that is your portion in life and in your struggle under the sun.*

> (CSB)

In other words, life is short, so enjoy life with the person you'll spend more of it with than anyone else. Through Craig

Groeschel's book *"From this Day Forward"* and through an Authentic Manhood Bible study, I have learned three ways we can make sure we're having fun in our marriage, and an equation I will never forget, that I hope you won't forget either!

- **Face-to-Face.** We must spend time together face-to-face enjoying each other's company. This is spending quality time together, intentionally listening and talking and looking each other in the eyes. Men like headlines and women like details, so it is spending time giving each other both of these things. Intimate and ongoing conversation is key to this, and like I have said many times before, a consistent, guarded, and faithful date night is a must!
- **Side-to-Side.** I want my wife to be my best friend, and my best friend is someone that I want to hang out with and spend time with. Do things with your spouse that they enjoy and try to identify some things that you enjoy doing together!
- **Back-to-Back.** You can't spend every moment together, so figure out some fun things and hobbies you enjoy doing personally and do those things as well. Have fun when you are separate so that you will enjoy the times you are together even more. Make sure you are doing things that your spouse trusts are good for you, and is okay with. Make sure you are communicating with your spouse and that they are secure while you are doing these things.
- **Face2Face + Side2Side + Back2Back = Belly Button2Belly Button.** I hope that this is an equation that you won't forget!

We all want our marriages to thrive, and I believe that they can thrive. If the grass looks greener somewhere else, remember it's time to water your own yard, because the other yard might be on top of a sewage drain. Invest in your marriage, and allow the Lord to do the work that only He can do as you grow in your relationship with Him first, and your relationship with your spouse second! Let's thrive!

- **Is there anything you need to forgive between you and your spouse?**
- **What characteristics of forgiveness do you struggle with the most?**
- **What can you do to have more fun this week? How can you get some time face-to-face with your spouse this week? What hobby can you do together side-to-side this week? What can you do to get some back-to-back alone time this week to allow God to refresh you?**

Appendix 1

Date Night Questions

1. 3 questions to ask every date night:
   a. What's on your heart and mind?
   b. What are you reading in the Bible and what is the Lord teaching you?
   c. What am I doing to be a blessing to you, and what could I do to be a bigger blessing to you?
2. What is one household chore you wish I would do?
3. What's one thing I can do this week to serve you?
4. What's one thing I have done in the last month that made you feel appreciated?
5. What's one thing that we're not currently doing as a couple that you wish we would do and why?
6. What's your favorite childhood memory, and what was your favorite hobby/game/toy?
7. What's your dream vacation? What was your favorite trip together?
8. What's your idea for a dream date night?
9. What's one thing you really want to do one day?
10. How many times a month would you like to have sex?
11. Who would you meet if you could meet anyone?
12. What is a game that you would love to play together during an at-home date night?
13. What's your most favorite movie, and what is your least favorite movie?
14. What's your favorite thing about marriage?

Appendix 2

Date Night Ideas

1. Movie Night!
2. At home on the porch/deck with cheese and wine.
3. Make s'mores around a fire pit!
4. Board Game Night—pick a fun game and make a bet on some chores!
5. Coffee Shop Date
6. Go to a toy store and have some fun!
7. Progressive Dinner Date—Different places for appetizer, entree, dessert.
8. Pizza-making and movie-watching night with popcorn.
9. Do something outdoors—lake, fishing, hiking, walk, etc.
10. Go watch a sunrise or sunset.
11. Go have a picnic.
12. Go play putt-putt, ride go-carts, go bowling, visit the batting cages or an arcade, etc.—do something competitive.
13. Go to a store and buy each other a gag gift.

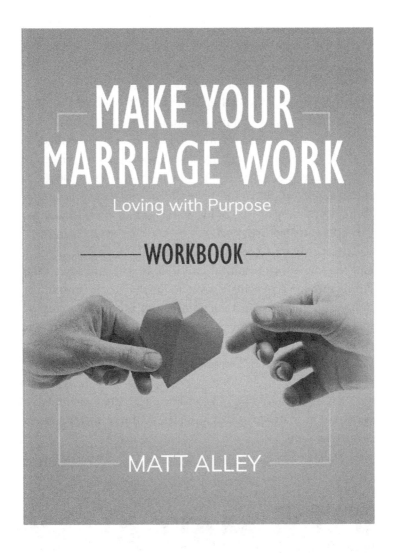

Download the supplemental study guide at
MattAlleyMinistries.com.

About the Author

Matt Alley is a follower of Christ, a husband, father, and pastor. He has been in ministry for 13 years, and a Campus Pastor at NewSpring Church Greenwood for over 7 years. Matt has a gifting, passion, and calling on his life to open up the Bible and teach it in a way that people can understand it and apply it to their lives. His personal mission is to advance the Kingdom of God by teaching Scripture and investing in marriages in order to see them thrive, and not just survive! He loves to speak about the Bible and to teach on marriage, and it was through teaching as well as his marriage and experiences that this book was birthed.

Matt is married to the love of his life, Erin Tench Alley, and they have two beautiful children, Mattie and Jase. Their family mission is to bring Heaven to Earth in their community by making disciples in their family and others, by being on mission to build the church together, and by having fun. The Alley's truly want to live their life loving God, loving others, loving God's Church, loving God's Word, and loving God's ways.

You can reach out to the author on Twitter @mattalley7, via email at matt@mattalleyministries.com, or at MattAlley-Ministries.com.

Made in the USA
Middletown, DE
01 June 2020